To my beloved Marguerite

Also by Pete Wallis

Are you okay? A practical guide to helping young victims of crime
IBSN 978 1 84905 098 2

What have I done? A victim empathy programme for young people
with Clair Aldington and Marian Liebmann
IBSN 978 1 84310 979 2

*Why me? A programme for children and young people who
have experienced victimisation*
with Shellie Keen and Tracie Lott
IBSN 978 1 84905 097 5

The pocket guide to restorative justice
with Barbara Tudor
IBSN 978 1 84310 629 6

Royalties from this book will be donated to the charity
SAFE! Support for Young People Affected by Crime
to help young people cope and recover following an
experience of victimisation (www.safeproject.org.uk).

UNDERSTANDING RESTORATIVE JUSTICE
How empathy can close the gap created by crime

Pete Wallis

First published in Great Britain in 2014 by

Policy Press
University of Bristol
6th Floor
Howard House
Queen's Avenue
Clifton
Bristol BS8 1SD
UK
t: +44 (0)117 331 5020
pp-info@bristol.ac.uk
www.policypress.co.uk

North America office:
Policy Press
c/o The University of Chicago Press
1427 East 60th Street
Chicago, IL 60637, USA
t: +1 773 702 7700
f: +1 773 702 9756
sales@press.uchicago.edu
www.press.uchicago.edu

© Policy Press 2014

British Library Cataloguing in Publication Data
A catalogue record for this book is available from the British Library

Library of Congress Cataloging-in-Publication Data
A catalog record for this book has been requested

ISBN 978 1 44731 742 5 paperback

Cover design by Soapbox
Front cover and all cartoon illustrations by Joseph Wilkins (josephwilkins.co.uk)
Printed and bound in Great Britain by Short Run Press, Exeter
Policy Press uses environmentally responsible print partners

Contents

List of figures and tables

Figures

Tables

Boxes

List of cartoons

About the author

Pete Wallis is a restorative justice practitioner with Oxfordshire's Youth Offending Service. He started his career as a teacher and has subsequently worked with young people with emotional and behavioural difficulties, ran a relapse prevention programme in a drug agency, managed a Quaker outreach centre with his wife, worked in a homeless day centre and with the Prison Phoenix Trust (a national charity that teaches yoga and meditation to prisoners). On joining the Youth Offending Service in 2000 he and colleagues established a restorative justice service and since then Pete has facilitated hundreds of restorative meetings between young people who offend and those they have harmed. He co-authored a pocket guide to restorative justice for practitioners and collaborated with two artists to publish a victim empathy programme called 'What Have I Done?'. Concerned for young people struggling to cope and recover following an experience of victimisation, Pete and his manager, Gordon Richardson, set up the charity SAFE! Support for Young People Affected by Crime in 2011. With Eric Fast, Pete designed the new restorative justice facilitator training course for the Youth Justice Board. He has organised and contributed to conferences, training events and talks on restorative justice, and recently became an assessor for the new Restorative Service Quality Mark. Inspired by his Quaker parents, Annette and Oscar, and his grandfather, Corder Catchpool, Pete is passionate about the benefits that restorative justice brings to individuals and society. He lives in Oxford with his wife Marguerite, and has two daughters, Thalia and Freya.

Acknowledgements

This book has arisen from my experience of facilitating restorative meetings over a number of years, coupled with some reading and numerous conversations with colleagues. Few of the ideas are new, and the book builds upon the inspiration and work of many people.

I am indebted to everyone who has helped with this book. Many people have read the manuscript at various stages and made suggestions that have improved it immensely. Incorporating everyone's comments has been very special, the wise voices of friends whispering in my ear as I have made changes to the text. As a result, the book has become truly collaborative, and I wish to thank everyone for their generosity.

I would like to thank my colleagues and management at Oxfordshire Youth Offending Service for the tremendous support and encouragement I have received over the years. I would also like to thank my mentors: Bonita Holland, Belinda Hopkins, Marian Liebmann, Gordon Richardson, Barbara Tudor, Mark Walters, Martin Wright and Howard Zehr. Thanks to my esteemed colleagues: Jo Brown (who coined the phrase 'resonant empathy'), Tasneem Clarke, Linda Darrall, Eric Fast and Katherine Stoessel. Thanks to my family: Annette, Oscar, Marguerite, Thalia, Freya, Julie and Pip. Thanks to Wilma Derksen, Lucy Jaffe (deputy director of Why Me?), Lizzie Nelson (ex-director of the Restorative Justice Council), Terry Brown (head of programme development at the Prison Fellowship) and Sian West (former prison governor and associate lecturer in criminology, University of Kent). Thanks to my wise friends and soulmates: Rebecca Baker, Sabita Banerji, Sandy Chubb, Denise Cullington, Lyn Ellis, John Gaynor, Bruno Guastalla, Shirley Harriott, Sister Elaine MacInnes, Penny Ormerod and Ed Wates. Thanks to Professor Dr Otmar Hagemann of Fachhochschule Kiel for sharing his ideas on the topic of empathy, to Professor John Braithwaite for kindly correcting the section on shame, guilt and empathy and to Bill Kerslake and Harry Potter for advice on criminal justice. Thanks to Joseph Wilkins for his brilliant cover illustration and cartoons. Thanks to Victoria Pittman, Alison Shaw, Laura Greaves and everyone at Policy Press.

Restorative justice has evolved over many years, and the theories, models and methods described here build upon the inspirational work of the early pioneers in this field, such as Tony Marshall in the UK and Mark Umbreit in the US. I have mentioned Belinda Hopkins, and her ideas were, in turn, developed from the work of Terry O'Connell and Marg Thorsborne in Australia. I make mention in the book of Marshall

Rosenberg's model of non-violent communication, and the restorative process also borrows from the fields of mediation, cognitive psychology and conflict resolution. I have not managed to find a source for the notion of 'parallel justice', a term that I heard at a conference some years ago. It is impossible to trace all the sources in the development of this swiftly evolving field, but if there are materials or ideas included here without proper credit to their author, please accept my apologies and alert the publisher so that this can be rectified.

Finally, I would like to acknowledge the courage of anyone choosing a restorative justice process. Special heartfelt thanks to Jo Berry, Ray and Vi Donovan, Claire Chung, Sari Stacey, Peter Woolf, and Marian Partington, who have shared their stories and improved this book immensely through their suggestions and insights. I have also drawn inspiration and some of the case studies from the book *After the crime* by Susan Miller (New York University Press, New York and London, 2011), which features remarkable stories of restorative meetings organised by Victim Voices Heard in Delaware and facilitated by executive director Kim Book.

Truax and Carkhuff, in *Toward effective counseling and psychotherapy: Training and practice* (Aldine, 1967), introduced the term 'empathy scale' in the context of the therapeutic relationship between therapist and client. Simon Baron-Cohen's book *Zero degrees of empathy* (Penguin, 2012) also contains the notion of a scale of empathy. In his research, Baron-Cohen used a questionnaire to establish an individual's 'empathy quotient', which, when applied to a large population, results in an 'empathy spectrum' with 'degrees of empathy' ranging from 0 to 6. Similar terms and concepts are also used here in the context of how empathy can develop between people engaging in a restorative process.

This book contains many stories and quotes from people who have been through a restorative process. Where these have already been published, they have been quoted verbatim and referenced in an endnote. Some of the case material has arisen from conversations with specific individuals who have kindly given their permission for their experience to be shared. I have also included some brief quotes and anecdotes based upon cases that I have been involved with professionally, which are not referenced. To preserve anonymity, the individuals' names and locations are not given, and the details of each case have been carefully altered to ensure that those involved cannot possibly be identified.

Any opinions expressed in this book are those of the author, and do not necessarily represent those of his employer.

Who is this book for?

This book has been written for a general readership, and requires no previous knowledge of restorative justice. It may be of particular interest to people who have been affected by crime, or those who have offended (or their relatives or friends), as well as people who work within criminal justice or for organisations supporting victims. It explores restorative justice as a journey, starting with the incident and moving through various stages and levels to the point where the people involved on both sides come together, seeking to resolve the crime and its aftermath. Each step is described in detail, so that by the end, the reader will have a firm understanding of the restorative justice process.

The book highlights the vital role of the skilled facilitator in ensuring that restorative justice is safe and effective. If you are new to the field, you may be surprised that the restorative process has an underlying logic, goes through clear procedures and stages, and has its own skill set, language and value base. This rigour is essential to enable the practitioner to feel confident when bringing people who have caused harm face to face with the people they have harmed. Restorative justice practitioners and their colleagues and managers may find in this book a fresh perspective and new insights to help them in their task. Finally, questions are raised for policymakers about how to reconcile restorative justice, which offers individuals space to explore their own needs and solutions, with a criminal justice system that often pulls in the opposite direction.

Although restorative approaches[1] are spreading into schools, neighbourhoods, housing, children's homes and many other settings, this book will focus on the use of restorative justice in the criminal context.

Note

[1] Belinda Hopkins introduced the term 'restorative approaches' to describe the profusion of new applications for restorative practice that are spreading out from its origin in criminal justice into ever-wider contexts, recognising that in non-criminal settings, such as schools, the term 'justice' can lead to confusion and is often deemed inappropriate. These are exciting developments. Not only will it help restorative justice if people – particularly the young – are already familiar with restorative approaches to conflict, and understand the notion that if you hurt someone it is natural to meet with them to sort it out, but restorative approaches can also be a powerful element of early intervention, catching pro-criminal behaviour before it becomes embedded. For information on restorative approaches in youth settings, see Belinda's website (www.transformingconflict.org).

Introduction

What is restorative justice?

At its heart, restorative justice is a conversation. It is a carefully facilitated conversation involving dialogue between people whose relationship has been damaged or destroyed as the result of a crime. Regardless of the nature of the crime or situation, or whether it takes place in the hours following the offence or follows months or even years of preparation, this conversation is likely to be highly charged. Sometimes, particularly in those cases where there is more serious harm, a restorative conversation can be extraordinary and life-changing.

Not all crimes occur between people who were previously known to one another, and a restorative conversation between people who are strangers and who are unlikely to meet again once the conversation has ended will have a different flavour to a restorative conversation between friends and acquaintances, family members or neighbours. Nevertheless, when any crime is committed, a new (and unwelcome) relationship begins.[1] A prolific offender may appear to be able to put aside their thoughts and feelings about each individual they have harmed. However, it is remarkable how clearly those memories can return given the right encouragement; they are buried but not forgotten. The person harmed is even less likely to forget. Even if they did not see the person responsible, they know the details about some of their actions and will often try to fill in the gaps with their imagination. The stranger has become 'the man who has packed his bags and moved in with you. He's living with you in your own home'.[2] After a crime, each side carries the other within, and more serious crimes establish a more profound connection.

A restorative conversation has the remarkable potential to loosen the grip of this damaging relationship. In cases where people were known to each other and will meet again, it can transform this relationship into one that is healthy and respectful, or even start or renew a friendship. During the process, people can be released from a burden that can otherwise, in some cases, blight lives.

Recognising the destruction caused by crime and its consequences, restorative justice pays close attention to everyone who has been affected – those who are harmed, those who are responsible, their supporters and their communities – understanding that justice will best be served when all those involved participate actively in finding a way forward. It is a process through which everyone affected by a crime is offered a safe opportunity to share their experience, hear one another's perspective on what happened, explore the impact of the offence on themselves and others, and work together towards resolution and healing. A successful restorative process has the power to reduce the social distance or 'gap' that results from crime.

Restorative conversations can be either direct, involving a carefully facilitated restorative meeting, or indirect, through messages, letters, video and so on. Box 0.1 outlines the key features of good restorative practice, which will be explored in this book.

Box 0.1: Key features of restorative justice

- There is thorough assessment and preparation.
- The process is facilitated with sensitivity and care by a trained restorative practitioner.
- Involvement is completely voluntary for those harmed and hopefully an active choice for the person who caused that harm.[3]
- The practitioner encourages openness and respect.
- While acknowledging that one has harmed the other, the practitioner avoids taking sides.

If the person responsible for the crime and those they harmed choose to come together in a restorative meeting, this will involve:

- agreeing who will be present;
- sitting in a circle;[4]
- negotiating ground rules about safety;
- creating an opportunity for honest, respectful listening;
- enabling everyone to tell their 'story' from their own perspective;
- hearing about the wider harm caused by the crime;
- exploring everyone's needs; and
- working together towards the future.

Successful restorative justice provides the setting for people to:

- be seen and acknowledged;
- voice their story and feel heard;
- hear and understand;
- help the other; and
- reach some level of healing.

As they engage in a restorative process, participants may not realise that they are being carefully supported and led through these steps. Restorative practitioners work to a carefully designed and well-grounded model, tried and tested over several decades of development. This demands skill, judgement and sensitivity.

Natural justice

If crime is seen as a conflict in which one person harms another, then the idea of arranging for these people to get together in a room and helping them find a mutual way forward is a sensible and, in many ways, natural thing to do. Restorative models of conflict resolution can be traced back to forms of justice used in many and varied cultures across the globe. The aboriginal community in Canada has used Healing Circles for centuries. The Palestinian practice of Sulha is an ancient form of justice for resolving serious offences, including murder. The Truth and Reconciliation processes that followed apartheid in South Africa, the Gacaca community courts in the wake of the genocides in Rwanda, the Mato Oput process in Uganda and the Commission for Reception, Truth and Reconciliation in East Timor were all based on local systems of justice with restorative elements, and the modern resurgence of interest in restorative justice is often traced back to Aboriginal practices in Australia and Māori custom in New Zealand.[5] It has been around forever. Most people understand and accept the logic. In some ways, it is like parenting: when siblings fight, we listen to both and seek to include both in finding solutions that address everyone's needs.

Although simple in principle, restorative justice can work with all categories of crime, from shoplifting through to the most serious offences, including murder, rape, hate crime and domestic violence, with research indicating that restorative justice leads to high levels of victim satisfaction and substantially reduces recidivism with some (but not all) people who commit crime, especially where those offences are more serious and/or violent.[6] In some cases, restorative justice is an alternative to the criminal justice process; in others, it forms part of or is in addition to a criminal procedure. For minor offences, a simple restorative process may be all that is required to resolve an incident, while more serious, sensitive and complex crimes require a range of interventions and resources to address the situation and meet everyone's needs, and for particular care to be given to assessment and preparation before a restorative meeting can be considered. Even so, the principles and features of restorative justice are the same for a case involving the theft of a chocolate bar from a supermarket and for a case involving an armed robbery; they are the same for a threatening text message and a murder.

Not all cases result in a restorative meeting, and not all restorative meetings result in healing or forgiveness. No particular outcome is guaranteed. Where a case involves a death, no process can restore things to how they were before. However, each restorative encounter where there is some form of communication will reach a certain level of 'restorativeness'. This book explores those levels, and considers how the practitioner can use their skills to enable participants to achieve the most restorative outcome from their situation.

Why the fascination with restorative justice?

Restorative justice is higher than it has ever been on the national agenda, with intense interest from the government, media, professionals and the public. In November 2013, Justice Minister Damian Green announced: 'At least £29million is being made available to Police and Crime Commissioners and charities to help deliver Restorative Justice for victims over the coming three years.'[7] An ICM telephone poll of 1,000 people, one month after the 2011 summer riots, found that:

> restorative measures, giving victims the opportunity to inform offenders of the harm caused and a say in how the offender can best make amends, attracted strong support. Nearly nine out of 10 people (88%) agreed that victims of theft and vandalism should be given the opportunity to inform offenders of the harm and distress they have caused.[8]

New initiatives such as neighbourhood justice panels and pre-sentence restorative justice are being promoted by the UK's Ministry of Justice, which is also investing in the delivery of restorative justice in youth justice, probation and prison services nationally.[9] The Matrix Report, an independent analysis of the economic benefits of restorative justice, estimates that a pre-court restorative justice scheme for young people who have offended would pay for itself over the first year, and during the course of two parliaments (10 years), such a scheme would save society £1 billion.[10]

There is a power and fascination about restorative work, because there is no one story, no one outcome. Every case is unique, involving carefully facilitated communication between people who may have little in common beyond sharing an incident that, in serious cases, neither will forget, and which may have changed their lives forever. It is also that rare phenomenon – a 'good news' story about crime where everyone wins. But there is more, something special that leads otherwise sober practitioners to start using words like 'magical' and 'transformative', and to describe a particular restorative meeting as a defining moment in their career. What is so extraordinary at the core, the heart, of restorative justice? This book attempts to delve deeply into the process to seek an answer.

Why do people choose restorative justice?

Crime violates people and relationships. Coming face to face in a restorative meeting is likely to be tough for everyone involved, and the more serious the crime, the tougher it is likely to be. Those who have been harmed often recognise that for the author of their crime, sitting across from them in a room explaining themselves is likely to be harder than any punishment the criminal justice system could impose. And the person harmed is also likely to arrive at the meeting feeling uncomfortable and apprehensive. Practitioners often ask in wonder why many people *do* choose to become involved: 'Why would you want to do it?'; 'Why would you want to face the person who harmed you?'; 'Why meet the person you harmed?'

At an adult prison a few years ago, a small handful of inmates were offered the chance of meeting the people they had harmed as part of a study into the efficacy of restorative justice (under the Justice Research Consortium, an international research project comprising a randomised control study of adult cases involving assault, robbery and personal theft).[11] The group were addressing a large room full of their fellow prisoners and talking about their restorative meetings. There was an excited buzz as almost all the prisoners in the room got caught up in the moment, and expressed a desire to meet the people they had harmed through their crimes. Hearing how powerful it had been for others got them thinking about all the people whose lives they had affected. Perhaps they were also keen to find something to do that they could feel good about.

There are also examples of people who have been harmed by crime literally fighting for the right to meet the person who harmed them. One case involved a young woman of 16 who urgently wanted to talk through what had occurred with her grandfather, who had just been released from custody having served a prison sentence for sexually abusing her as a child. Her father refused to meet with the restorative justice worker, the probation victim liaison officer supervising the grandfather was opposed to the idea and her mother wasn't too keen, worried that it was stirring up bad things in the family (although this was never confirmed, the restorative justice worker had a hunch that the young woman's mother might also have been abused, and that her resistance stemmed from having been unable to process the experience). The young woman was forced to wait for this meeting until she was 18, and even then, she had a major struggle with the authorities before the meeting was arranged – against both her parents' wishes. The meeting went well, and she was able to say what she needed to say to her grandfather.

What is the pull that makes people go to these lengths? Are they seeking release? Redemption? Healing?

A magnetic pull

Here is the mystery and fascination of restorative justice. The process tends to naturally draw people in. It is as if a knot of entanglement is created by a crime. Lives became irrevocably entwined, and those involved can't let it go. They sense that this bond can be loosened only through the healing power of a restorative meeting, in a process that has empathy at its heart.

The importance of empathy

Empathy has been described as 'the capacity to think and feel oneself into the inner life of another person'.[12] When we empathise, we are trying to understand, as well as possible, what the other person is experiencing, and to communicate this to them.

Empathy is a notoriously complex topic, and one that is of interest to a range of disciplines, including philosophy, aesthetics, psychology, neuroscience and restorative justice. Because it is not an intellectual quality, it is difficult to define precisely in words. In 1907, Lipps called empathy 'a psychological resonance phenomenon'.[13] His notion of 'inner imitation' reflects contemporary neuroscientific research into so-called 'mirror neurons' and the finding that 'the perception of another person activates similar neurons in the subject and the target'.[14] The initial trigger for empathy appears to be an unconscious and automatic mirroring of another person's emotional state, in which one person reads and responds to verbal or non-verbal cues from another.

Empathy has three elements: identifying with what another person is feeling (affective empathy); assessing the reasons for their emotional state (cognitive empathy); and taking action in response. As we empathise, our focus changes from thinking of ourselves to thinking of the other; from self-centred to other-centred. For example, when someone we love is ill, our concern about our own problems disappears, and our attention becomes focused on them. In the process, our sense of separation from that person breaks down. We don't lose ourselves entirely, and some distance and self-awareness remains because we know that it is not 'me' suffering, but as we empathise, we are recognising suffering in the other person and connecting it to our own experience.

Empathy is normally thought about as a one-way thing, with a subject and a target – one person (the subject) expressing empathy for another (the target). In restorative justice, the starting point is a crime, during which one side deliberately harms the other; one is therefore suffering as a direct result of the other's selfish actions. People naturally start off poles apart, and at the moment of the offence, empathy between the parties is quite often totally absent. Caught in a potentially life-changing conflict, they may enter the process – and sometimes the restorative justice meeting room – in a position of antipathy, possibly harbouring a wish for the other person to be punished, harmed or even dead. As the restorative process unfolds and people's stories start to be shared, empathy can arise equally for both sides, particularly if it becomes clear that the person responsible is also suffering (even if this is only because they are learning about the extent of the damage they caused). The magic at the heart of restorative justice is this dynamic and unexpected unfolding of empathy between people, often communicated non-verbally as well as verbally, through a smile, a handshake or a hug. It is not unheard of for people to enter the room fearing or even hating the other person, and leave expressing a hope for their well-being, healing and happiness. What other process can generate this level of empathy, all in under an hour?

Empathy is the driver for the restorative process, and the impact of a restorative meeting is largely dependent upon the degree to which those involved can start to empathise with one another. This gives a new twist to the mirroring aspect of empathy, as a dynamic process can develop in which each person is both expressing suffering and responding to suffering in the other. That someone is suffering may be obvious from the person's demeanour, but often, particularly when we are bound up in our own drama and suffering, we need to be encouraged to become open to hearing about the suffering of others. The restorative process does this by giving everyone a chance to talk about their own experience and feelings and by encouraging them to listen carefully to the experience and feelings of others.

To get to the heart

Restorative justice is a journey; one in which increasing insight and empathy allow growth and healing to arise from the painful and negative experience of a crime. In fact, it involves two interconnected journeys, with two separate parties moving inexorably towards one another. Echoing Lipps, I am calling this dynamic process *resonant empathy*. Restorative practitioners often talk about 'movement', and an interesting aspect of this resonant empathy is that often neither can advance very far without movement from the other. Moreover, every small increase in empathy from one side can lead to an increase in empathy from the other – like the movement in one violin string generating resonance in the other strings.

The resonant empathy model offered here attempts to get to the core of this restorative process, to illuminate its mystery and power. There are various levels of empathy, and this book introduces an empathy scale (Figure 0.1), which starts at the bottom with low or even negative empathy (antipathy), rising through various stages to the highest levels of empathy. At the bottom, the primary concern is for one's own needs (to have hurt acknowledged, to feel seen, to be heard), while as empathy rises, the focus shifts to the needs of others (to help, to heal).

Figure 0.1: The empathy scale

LOW   HIGH

The model is designed to chart the restorative journey: starting with the offence itself (Empathy Level Zero); entry into the criminal justice system (Empathy Level One); initial discussions with the parties involved, exploring those not infrequent situations where there is little or no scope for anything restorative (and even a danger that things could be made worse) (Empathy Level Two); indirect communication and the start of the restorative conversation (Empathy Level Three); the heart of the restorative meeting (Empathy Level Four); and finally the themes that make this process potentially literally life–changing for those involved (Empathy Level Five). Each level will be explored as the book progresses.

This book contains first-hand accounts from people who have experienced some of the most serious crimes, including rape and the murder of loved ones, and chosen to meet the person responsible in a restorative meeting. In sharing these inspirational stories, it is not my intention to imply that restorative justice is a model or an outcome to which everyone who has been harmed by crime must aspire. Everyone reacts differently following a crime, and Chapter Nine explains that a particular combination of circumstances is required for a restorative meeting to be possible and appropriate.

A note on terminology

To illustrate the restorative process simply, most of this book has been written as if there are only two people involved in a crime: 'the person responsible' and 'the person harmed'. It is recognised that most criminal cases are more complex than this, involving more than just one person causing harm and one person harmed, while, in many cases, lines of responsibility are not clear-cut, with both parties to some extent sharing the blame for what happened. The role of supporters is also crucial in restorative justice meetings and is explored in Chapter Ten.

Where possible, the words 'offender' and 'victim' are avoided in favour of 'the person responsible' and 'the person harmed'. While it makes the text more cumbersome, the problem with 'offender' and 'victim' is that they are labels that attach a single identity to the human being who had that experience. With more than one in five of us experiencing crime or offending each year,[15] we are talking about real-life individuals in our houses, streets and neighbourhoods. When you join a queue at the supermarket, you are quite likely to be behind someone who has at some point committed a crime and someone who has at some point been harmed by a crime, simply getting on with their ordinary lives.

The term 'practitioner' is loosely employed to encompass a wide range of professionals and volunteers who organise and facilitate restorative justice. They may be probation officers, youth offending team workers, police, prison staff, referral panel volunteers, neighbourhood justice panel volunteers, mediators or dedicated restorative justice or victim liaison workers.

The word 'healing' is used freely in the text. Research indicates that involvement in a restorative justice meeting can have positive health benefits for those involved, which I believe justifies the use of the term. The healing potential of restorative justice is explored in Chapter Thirteen.

Words like 'transformative' and 'magical' (which may seem more suited to a Harry Potter film trailer than a book on criminal justice) also creep in occasionally. Many of the case examples in the book concern restorative meetings following serious crimes, and often a restorative process is rather pedestrian and functional (although still helpful) and might not justify those lofty terms, but there *is* something that happens in a particularly powerful restorative meeting that brings out this kind of language from practitioners and sometimes from participants themselves. In writing this book, these phrases have been checked with people who have been through a restorative meeting following very serious crimes, and they insist that they describe their experience accurately.

Notes

[1] The word 'relationship' is used here in a restorative justice context meaning a connection between people, without intending any of the undertones of friendship or love that are often associated with the term. Restorative justice pioneer Howard Zehr has described crime as 'a violation of people and interpersonal relationships' (Zehr, H. [2002] *The little book of restorative justice*, Intercourse, PA: Good Books, p 19). A crime creates a connection that leaves those involved in a negative relationship, which may remain harmful if there is no resolution.

[2] Miller, S. (2011) *After the crime*, New York, NY: New York University Press, p 128.

[3] The degree to which the restorative process is voluntary for the person responsible is explored in Chapter Eight.

[4] Chapter Ten explores why the circle is so important in restorative justice. In a prison setting, where chairs may already be fixed to the floor, a circle is not always possible, although everyone will be together in the room.

[5] Marian Liebmann's book *Restorative justice: How it works* (Jessica Kingsley Publishers, 2007) has an excellent chapter on the history of restorative justice.

[6] Sherman, L. and Strang, H. (2007) *Restorative justice: The evidence*, London: The Smith Institute.

[7] www.gov.uk/government/news/new-victims-funding-for-restorative-justice

[8] www.prisonreformtrust.org.uk/PressPolicy/News/vw/1/ItemID/143

[9] You can keep up to date with developments via the RJC (Restorative Justice Council) (www.restorativejustice.org.uk).

[10.] www.restorativejustice.org.uk/restorative_justice_works/

[11.] Shapland, J., Atkinson, A., Colledge, E., Dignan, J., Howes, M., Johnstone, J., Pennant, R., Robinson, G. and Sorsby, A. (2004) 'Implementing restorative justice schemes (Crime Reduction Programme): a report on the first year', Home Office Online Report 32/04, Home Office, London.

[12.] Heinz Kohut, quoted in Stepansky, P. and Goldberg, A. (eds) (1984) *Kohut's legacy: Contributions to self psychology*, Hillsdale, NJ: The Analytic Press, p 82.

[13.] Lipps, T. (1907) 'Das Wissen von Fremden Ichen', *Psychologische Unters-uchungen*, vol 1, pp 694–722.

[14.] Stueber, K. (2013) 'Empathy' (first published 31 Mar 2008; substantive revision 14 February 2013; http://plato.stanford.edu/entries/empathy/).

[15.] According to the 2010/11 British Crime Survey 21.59% of adults in England and Wales were victims of at least one crime in the 12 months prior to interview and according to the Ministry of Justice over the same period around 640,000 people who offended were cautioned, convicted (excluding immediate custodial sentences) or released from custody. Sources: 'Crime in England and Wales 2010/11: Findings from the British Crime Survey and police recorded crime (2nd edition)', edited by Rupert Chaplin, John Flatley and Kevin Smith, July 2011; and 'Ministry of Justice Proven Re-offending Statistics Quarterly Bulletin, April 2010 to March 2011, England and Wales' (www.justice.gov.uk/statistics/reoffending/proven-re-offending).

Part One
Empathy Level Zero: hurting

If we could read the secret history of our enemies, we would find in each man's life a sorrow and a suffering enough to disarm all hostility.

(Henry Wadsworth Longfellow)[1]

CHAPTER ONE

Crime and unhappiness

Crime and the rule of law

Laws are rules created by judges or parliament to enable society to function. Originally, the law was probably little more than custom, which was then codified and issued by kings; in fact, the earliest decipherable writing of any length was a code of law (the Code of Hammurabi, a Babylonian tablet with text outlining 282 laws, dates back to about 1772 BC).[2] There are rules backed up by law everywhere around us. This is generally a good thing, for example, ensuring that we stop at traffic lights and avoid smoking in enclosed public places and on railway platforms. There is usually an assumption that laws are necessary, fair and just, which matches reality 90% of the time – but perhaps not entirely. Crime is a relative rather than an absolute concept, which is defined by a society and changes over time. Homosexuality was a crime in the UK until 1967 and remains an offence in 76 countries around the world (five of which punish homosexual acts with the death penalty),[3] while non-consensual sex within marriage did not constitute rape until 1991. Drug legislation fails to encompass alcohol, which is the most dangerous intoxicant of all, and the only one that is regularly related to violent crime (if alcohol were to be invented tomorrow and imported from South America, it would instantly become a Class A drug). For all its faults, the rule of law is a guarantee that wrongdoing will be addressed in a way that is independent and outside of ourselves as individuals, and this code is what makes society possible. We realise its merits if we consider what would happen if it wasn't there.

There are a bewildering number of laws that permeate every aspect of our lives – the Labour government famously broke the record by introducing 3,506 new laws during its last year in office (2010)[4] – covering everything from the legal obligations of employing a nanny to the ownership of washed-up whales (they belong to the sovereign). This book will focus on behaviour that is both unlawful and leads to someone being directly harmed as a result, recognising that 'crime' and 'harm' are not always synonymous, and there are crimes (like driving without a licence or smoking cannabis) where it isn't possible to name an individual who has been harmed. While acknowledging that white-collar and corporate crimes also harm individuals and warrant a restorative approach, the book addresses offences committed more directly against the person, such as domestic burglary and assault.[5] It accepts the need to debate and criticise our current laws and legal system, but the emphasis here is on how society deals with those who break that law.

Why do people commit crime?

Decisions we make in life are the product of a myriad of factors, past and present, all of which lead us towards making a particular choice in any given moment. Consider the last time you bought margarine. Reaching for that particular brand on the shop shelf might have been carefully planned to meet a particular need, or could have been an impulsive act – you happened to see it prominently on display and took it without thinking. You may have gone for the cheapest or the most expensive, the tastiest or the healthiest option, dependent perhaps on how much cash you had on you. Your mood, living circumstances, previous choices, gender, age, background, habits or influences from childhood could all have been factors; that is, your choice will have been dependent upon what happened in the minutes, days, months and years before you arrived at the margarine display. Perhaps, if you weren't shopping alone, the people you were with persuaded you to follow their advice on which brand to choose. Maybe you were simply doing what you were told by your parents, flatmates or partner, or whoever it was who wrote 'Make sure it's Flora' on the shopping list. Your choice in that moment might have been premeditated, targeted, impulsive or random – or the only option available to you on the shelf. Margarine manufacturers and supermarkets invest heavily in researching the complex reasons behind your choice.

It's a big leap from choosing margarine to committing crime, but the example does demonstrate how even our smallest choices are dictated by context, circumstance, personality and environment. Similarly, there are many reasons that lead people to commit crime. Each criminal event is unique and results from a complex array of issues, as depicted in Figure 1.1.[6] People who commit crimes are often able to identify these factors themselves (see Figure 1.2).

The Italian criminologist Cesare Lombroso (1835–1909) famously (and incorrectly) concluded that skull measurements provided evidence of genetic criminality. Since then, criminologists have written and theorised at length about the origins of criminal activity, citing, for example, weak social bonds (social control theory), socio-economic

Figure 1.1: Analysis of factors and pathways contributing to criminal events and behaviours

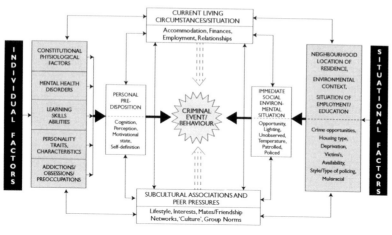

Figure 1.2: The conflict tree

Note: During a victim empathy course, Liam reflects on the factors that led to his crime. These include: Past factors ('upbringing'); External influences and peer pressure ('mates'); Circumstances immediately preceding and triggering the crime ('He said hurtful things'); and Internal factors ('pride'). The leaves are his reflections on the consequences of his behaviour

Source: Reproduced with kind permission from Wallis, P., Aldington, C. and Liebmann, M. (2010) *What have I done? A victim empathy programme for young people*, London: Jessica Kingsley Publishers.

pressures (strain theory), structural inequality (conflict theory), geographical factors (the Chicago School) and learned behaviour from criminal subcultures (differential association theory), adding in factors to do with race, ethnicity and cultural marginalisation. Some even argue that we are all potential criminals but that moral choices stop us from committing crime.

Against this complexity, Bo Lozoff[7] asserted boldly during a talk I attended in 1994 that 'All crime arises from unhappiness'. It is a sweeping statement that, like most generalisations, doesn't completely hold up to scrutiny. Many crimes relate to unhappiness only in the most tangential way (although a rival theory that relates crime to high rather than low self-esteem has been refuted through research).[8] Greed motivates many perpetrators, particularly in white-collar crimes, and prejudice, contempt for others and alcohol (which can facilitate crime) may all be causative factors. It is also wrong to suggest that everyone committing a crime is the victim of circumstances beyond their control, and therefore bear no moral responsibility for their acts. With all these caveats, there is still a grain of truth in Bo's comment. People who commit crime often (not always) have a well of unhappiness arising from unresolved lack, loss, rejection or abuse, although many will not have consciously acknowledged this.

In the 1990s, I helped facilitate a groupwork programme for men on probation who had been convicted of 'joyriding' – a crime not immediately associated with unhappiness. Participants were invited to draw a 'life graph', where the horizontal axis went from birth to the present and the vertical axis from deeply unhappy at the bottom to ecstatically happy at the top (see Figure 1.3). The example drawn on the flipchart showed typical ups (getting a new job, having a baby) and downs (losing someone special, breaking up with a partner), with an average state of happiness somewhere in the middle. I recall one group where the young men (without looking at one another's graphs) all crammed their lines and lives in the inch or so *beneath* the bottom axis – presumably feeling that their lives all belonged in a zone below deep unhappiness. Moreover, without any prompting, they all identified a negative life event immediately preceding their offence. This confirms research which shows that crime often follows loss, which was certainly true for this group. One study of 200 young offenders found that 57% had experienced bereavement or traumatic loss.[9] Unresolved grief is a significant risk factor for turning young people to offending.

Figure 1.3: An example of a life graph

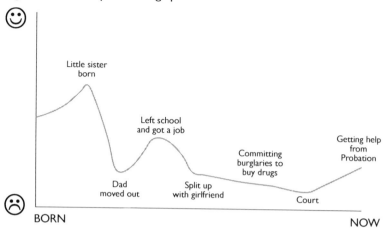

When crime arises from a place of unhappiness, it is sometimes possible to trace its origin to an earlier experience of victimisation – often far back in childhood. Some families seem caught in a cycle of crime that goes back generations, and for many, episodes of committing crime are punctuated by experiences of being victimised. One study found that 50% of young people who had committed an offence in the previous 12 months had also been the victim of a personal crime in the same period, compared with 19% of those who had not committed an offence,[10] while in another study, more than two thirds of serious

Cartoon 1.1: Breaking the cycle

young offenders disclosed childhood abuse.[11] Speaking out in 2002 against a tide of political rhetoric about being 'tough on crime', Sir David Ramsbotham said of young people in custody:

> Most have grown up in impoverished circumstances in socially deprived areas within chaotic, struggling families; many have had damaging periods in local authority care, many have been badly let down by the education system, many have faced racial and other forms of discrimination, many have been physically and sexually abused. Anyone who has worked with these children knows the painful truth ... and that those who portray young offenders as clever immoral thugs taking advantage of a soft system could not be wider off the mark. Select at random any inmate of a young offender institution, and you will almost certainly find a heart-breaking history of personal misery, professional neglect and lost opportunities.[12]

This makes for a powerful case for early intervention to prevent future offending (see Box 1.1).

Box 1.1: Young people in custody: a catalogue of misery

Government statistics[13] show that if you randomly choose 100 young people aged 15–18 from youth custody, on average:

- 44 will have a history of local authority care;
- 75 will have lived with someone other than their own parents at some point in their lives and 45 will have lived in unsuitable accommodation in the 12 months before sentencing;
- 25 will have suffered violence at home;
- 55 will not have had access to full-time education prior to custody and 28 will have had no education at all prior to custody;
- 50 will have literacy and numeracy levels below that of an 11 year old and 25 below that of an average seven year old;
- 85 will show signs of personality disorder and 31 will have mental health needs, including depression, anxiety and post-traumatic stress;
- 72 will have used cannabis daily in the 12 months before their arrest and 69 drank alcohol or used drugs in order to think less about their problems; and
- 60 will have been in custody before and six will have been in five times or more.

The link between empathy and offending

Empathy, by definition, stops us from harming another person, and in order for a crime to be possible, the person responsible must have no empathy for the person they are harming, at least at the moment the crime is committed. Loss of empathy can be temporary or long-term.

Simon Baron-Cohen, Professor of Developmental Psychopathology at the University of Cambridge, has designed a questionnaire to determine an individual's ability to empathise and uses this to create an 'empathy spectrum', divided into 'degrees' of empathy. Everyone sits somewhere on a continuum, which takes the form of a bell-shaped curve or normal distribution (see Figure 1.4). People at the left-hand end of the curve with zero degrees of empathy are able to commit acts of great cruelty with no remorse. At the other end of the spectrum are people with high degrees of empathy, where deliberately harming others would be unthinkable.

Figure 1.4: The empathy curve

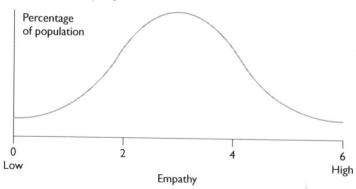

Source: Baron-Cohen, S. (2012) *Zero degrees of empathy*, London: Penguin. Reproduced with kind permission of the author.

Baron-Cohen found that people with certain personality disorders show 'zero degrees' of empathy, and his research has indicated that these individuals typically experienced trauma as a result of early abuse, insecure attachment and neglect, which interrupted the development of healthy empathy. Baron-Cohen has identified a neurological 'circuit' where empathy is located, and shown that prolonged exposure to stress and trauma can lead to specific regions in the brain becoming underactive or abnormal. For some people, low or zero empathy develops into a long-term and stable trait arising out of years of extreme childhood unhappiness. This would chime with the high percentage of people in custody who have a personality disorder (Box 1.1), although these findings must be interpreted carefully. We know that large sections of the population experience childhood abuse and don't fit into this pattern, and, indeed, that many people who survive abuse are deeply empathetic.

People with low or 'zero empathy' are not predestined to offend, and not all people who offend have personality disorders. For many, the loss of empathy is short-term, and may relate to a specific situation or person. The trigger can still arise from unhappiness, and an offence may be committed when an individual feels inadequate, ashamed, judged, hard done by, threatened or vengeful, or when they are irritated or angry. Being drunk, tired, stressed or impatient can lead to a sudden drop in empathy, and group pressures and competitive situations may also be significant factors.

It is harder to empathise with another person and easier to deliberately harm them when we are unhappy, because unhappiness feeds our personal drama, focusing our attention on the self. Moreover, the trigger for the feelings that lead someone to offend may be totally unrelated to the person they harm: 'When our empathy is switched off, we are solely in the "I" mode. In such a state we relate only to things, or to people as if they were just things.'[14]

Identifying an explanation for crime that may be rooted in unhappiness – current or historic – doesn't excuse or condone harmful actions (a point many perpetrator's make themselves in restorative meetings) or deny the anguish and pain they result in. However, to some degree, it is what makes restorative justice work. Often, the most pressing question for people hurting following a crime is 'Why did you do it?' Learning about the perpetrator's unhappiness can provide at least a partial explanation. It can also unlock empathy in the person harmed, a point that is further developed in later chapters.

Notes

[1.] Longfellow, Henry Wadsworth ([1909] 2013) *Kavanagh: The Indian summer, the bald eagle, and driftwood* (Vol. 3). London: Forgotten Books.

[2.] See Potter, H. (2014) *A brief's history of the law*, Woodbridge: Boydell and Brewer. This book will be a history of the English common law expanding on the research Harry Potter did when presenting for the BBC series 'The strange case of the law'.

[3.] Ilga.org

[4] www.bbc.co.uk/news/uk-politics-13569604

[5] Focusing on young people harmed by crime, *Are you okay?* (Wallis, P., 2010, London: Jessica Kingsley Publishers) has a section outlining the technical definitions of all crimes against the person, including the impact of those crimes and what might help those affected in their recovery.

[6] This figure is unpublished, and has been reproduced with kind permission from Dr Colin Roberts.

[7] Bo Lozoff was the founder of the Prison Ashram Project in the US and author of *We're all doing time*, Lozoff, B. (1985) *We're all doing time: A guide for getting free*, 16th printing 2006, Durham, NC: Human Kindness Foundation.

[8] Ocer, C. (2006) 'The criminal offending–self-esteem nexus: which version of the self-esteem theory is supported?', *The Prison Journal*, vol 86, no 3, pp 344–63.

[9] Day, C., Hibbert, P. and Cadman, S. (2008) *A literature review into children abused and/or neglected prior custody*, London: YJB.

[10] Roe, S. and Ashe, J. (2008) *Young people and crime: Findings from the 2006 Offending, Crime & Justice Survey*, London: Home Office.

[11] Williams, B. (1999) *Working with victims of crime*, London: Jessica Kingsley Publishers.

[12] Sir David Ramsbotham (2002) *Rethinking child imprisonment: A report on young offenders institutions*, London: Children's Rights Alliance for England, p 5.

[13] Whittle, J. (2013) 'Youth justice and the law: a practitioner's handbook', Resettlement UK CIC.

[14] Baron-Cohen, S. (2012) *Zero degrees of empathy*, London: Penguin, p 6.

CHAPTER TWO

The gap caused by crime

The starting point for the person responsible

With few exceptions (a mother stealing because her child is hungry, a youth who uses disproportionate violence during a fight to protect a friend), committing a crime is a self-centred occupation, even if it is done in a group. During the offence, the primary concern of the person responsible is for Number One, and in the immediate aftermath, they are usually preoccupied with avoiding the consequences. In the words of Kelvin, who committed a string of burglaries, 'The only person I cared about was myself, and everyone else could go to hell.'[1] While it is fair to say that some people instantly regret what they have done, and some may even feel remorse straight after the event (a clear sign that their empathy lapse was brief), it is rare for people who commit crimes to hand themselves in, unless for selfish reasons. Thinking about our own offending, our first thought when we have flown past a speed camera (exceeding the speed limit), stolen a pen from an office (theft) or left dog poop in the park (breach of a local Dog Control Order) is likely to be not instant regret at the real or potential harm we have caused others, but a hope that we will get away with it without having to face any potentially embarrassing consequences.

People committing crime usually know at some level that they are causing harm – there is a warning bell ringing away somewhere inside their head, but it is suppressed or ignored. An obvious example is people who commit property offences to pay for drugs. Their desire for a fix drowns out their inner bell, and they choose to steal, often from their family and friends – the people they love the most – again and again.

Some career criminals actively train themselves to ignore the bell. Using a process that Gresham Sykes and David Matza termed 'neutralisation', they suppress their usual values to enable them to commit acts that their 'inner protests' would normally proscribe, even though they know what the consequences will be in advance.[2] Others may have been taught offending as a way of life from an early age, such that committing crime is so intimately connected to their identity that they fail to recognise that what happened in the past does not have to be continually played out in their future.

Sometimes, there is a louder noise that drowns out the bell – the need to be respected by peers. Gang initiation ceremonies may require unprovoked violence, which is sometimes directed at someone completely random, as was the case with Junior Henry, the teenager who stabbed a student at the Notting Hill Carnival in 2011. To do so, he must have deliberately suppressed any feelings for the young man he stabbed, must have avoided looking into his eyes – in fact, avoided seeing him as a person at all. I remember a young man describing how when committing robberies, he would just "go for it, put a lot of violence into it" in order to scare the person he was attacking. If he didn't, he explained, his mates would laugh at him and call him a "pussy".

In the animal kingdom, it is rare for an animal to kill other members of their species. Grossman (1995)[3] argues that humans also have an instinctive aversion to killing fellow humans, pointing out that some soldiers shoot to miss. In 1947, Brigadier General S.L.A Marshall made the controversial claim that only 15–20% of American riflemen were willing to use their weapons during World War II.[4] Although his 'combat fire ratio' has since been questioned,[5] Marshall's assertion led to modern armies employing Pavlovian and operant conditioning to enable soldiers to overcome any resistance to violence. Grossman is concerned that civilian society, by allowing graphic violence to be depicted in the media (citing interactive video games as a particular threat), is inadvertently replicating military conditioning techniques, which he believes could have a causative link with violent crime.[6]

Figure 2.1 shows an empathy scale for the person who caused harm. We have defined empathy as our ability to recognise and respond to the emotional state of the other person, and at the bottom is where most (though not all) perpetrators start – with thought only for the self, none for the other.

Figure 2.1: Starting point on the empathy scale for the person responsible

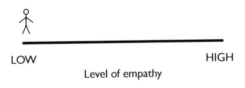

LOW   HIGH

Level of empathy

After the event, many people who have caused harm remain in denial, convincing themselves with their self-talk: 'I wasn't there'; 'I didn't do it'; 'It wasn't my fault'; 'I had no choice'; 'I was forced to do it'; 'I couldn't help it'; 'It wasn't so bad'; 'No one was hurt'. They may run away, get away with it and remain in their delusional bubble. If caught, they may still try to minimise, justify, deny, excuse and shift the blame for what happened.[7] They may put pressure on those they hurt not to report – to 'grass' – which is frequently a ploy to avoid facing the consequences of actions they know were wrong by deflecting blame on to the person they harmed. These avoidance strategies, in which people carefully construct a structure of innocence to justify their harmful behaviour, are natural impulses. We all use defence mechanisms in order to seek refuge from shameful feelings, to feel worthwhile. It is normal to play down our culpability, and attempt to avoid the consequences of behaviour we aren't proud of.

The starting point for the person harmed

For some people, being the victim of a minor crime may be experienced as a 'survivable nuisance', involving not much more than replacing credit cards or putting a lock on the garage door (although, on some level, every crime erodes our sense of trust in the community we live among, and our faith in other people). Crimes that cut more deeply can come as a sudden and shocking moment in time for the person harmed. Their familiar and safe world is turned upside down, their lives are changed forever.

Crime can really hurt. It attacks our most basic sense of self, who we are and what our world is like. It takes away our control – we are powerless to stop something horrible happening. There are several layers of consequence. The person harmed may suffer a drop in self-confidence and self-esteem, and be left feeling sullied, ashamed and humiliated. In grave crimes, the wounding can be profound and may cause severe emotional injury, which can develop into 'post-traumatic stress' (PTS). This is the name given to a range of disturbing psychological symptoms that arise in response to a traumatic experience, which may include triggers,[8] flashbacks, panic attacks, hyper-vigilance, intrusive recall and sleep disturbance. A young man described to me how he lay in his bed one night paralysed with fear. Light from the street was coming through a slit where the curtains didn't quite meet, and it looked like the blade used to threaten him during a street robbery. If left untreated, PTS can become chronic and develop into 'post-traumatic stress disorder' (PTSD), a longer-term condition that is difficult to treat.

People experience crime differently, and even seemingly minor crimes can affect people deeply depending on the circumstances. A woman who was terminally ill in bed was devastated to learn that someone had vandalised the windscreen wiper of her car. She was too ill to ever drive again, but this random and thoughtless act felt particularly personal and cruel.

People who feel a crime deeply usually start off in a state of shock. Then follows denial: 'This can't be happening to me.' Then anger. This they may turn in on themselves – which can lead to self-blame – or focus on the other, when anger can translate into vengeful feelings: a desire to hurt the person who hurt them. Even if you are the Dalai Lama, if your wallet is taken or your house broken into, your very first thought will not be: 'Oh, well I guess they must really need the money.' If your bike is stolen, you won't immediately conclude that someone was probably running late for something vital.

Cartoon 2.1: Ah, bless...

When a crime is committed, the message from the person responsible is: 'I count and you don't, my needs trump your needs. I can use and abuse you as an object with no respect for you as a person.' It is therefore quite natural if people who have been targeted and attacked have little or no empathy. They may have to think of themselves first for safety reasons, fortifying themselves physically or mentally in readiness for a future attack. Many will slide off the bottom of the empathy scale altogether, particularly if a loved one has been harmed or killed, when the strength of the rage that arises can come as quite a shock. A woman whose son was knocked down by a 'joyrider' said that she would quite happily run the man down if she saw him on the pavement – and then reflected on how, as a mother of three, she would never have thought she could have those feelings. Marian Partington, whose sister Lucy was murdered by Fred and Rosemary West, writes: 'Until then I hadn't thought of myself as a murderous person, but at that moment I was capable of killing. In other words I was not separate from the Wests'.[9] Vi Donovan, whose son Christopher was killed by a gang, described the days that followed:

> All I could feel was rage and anger. I went home and I smashed my kitchen up. I just lost it completely, because I was riding on all of that rage. I was drinking a cup of poison and hoping it would poison them, and it wasn't doing anything, it was just hurting me.[10]

Without a safe outlet, this rage can become misdirected towards family, friends and others.

In the aftermath of the crime, if you were to consider how much empathy the person harmed has for the person responsible for harming them, it is a fair guess that this will probably be close to zero (bearing in mind that there will be exceptions). Figure 2.2 shows the empathy scale for the person harmed.

Figure 2.2: Starting point on the empathy scale for the person harmed

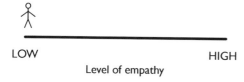

LOW   HIGH

Level of empathy

Two categories of crime

In restorative justice terms, there are two categories of crime. In the first category, there is some element of shared responsibility for what happened. Imagine two people getting into a fight. It starts off fairly evenly in terms of who throws the first few punches, but leads to one entering the criminal justice system as 'offender' and the other as 'victim'. This could be because one ends up seriously hurt, although it could just as easily have been the other person being taken away in an ambulance; or one reports it to the police and so is the 'victim', while the other doesn't (or does so later than the first) and becomes the 'offender'; or a witness, who may not have seen how the conflict started, perceives only one to be the aggressor. In this category of crime, both sides share some responsibility for what happened, and in some cases, responsibility can be almost evenly divided – even if from one moment to the next, one person picks up the 'offender' label and the other becomes the 'victim'. In some cases, the current offence is committed in retaliation for a previous grievance, to settle old scores or to right a perceived wrong – all of which can further blur the issue of culpability.

In the second category, responsibility lies solely with one side. Someone is targeted at random by a pickpocket, is mugged at a bus stop, burgled or groomed over the Internet and then sexually assaulted. Sometimes, the person harmed may have been unwise – leaving the keys in the ignition of their car; forgetting to close a bathroom window; leaving their bag on their table when they went to the bar to order drinks – but they did nothing wrong to have ended up in their position. Ironically, people harmed through random crimes – those who bear no responsibility for what happened – frequently blame themselves, playing events over and over again to see what they might have done to cause it to happen or make it worse than it might have been, perhaps to gain a sense of control over the incident.

Both are likely to start at the bottom of the empathy scale

Whether responsibility for what happened is equally shared or belongs exclusively with one side (while recognising that the moral position in these contrasting situations may be poles apart), and whether or not they were previously known to each other, in one respect, everyone's experience converges. Immediately following the crime, both the person harmed and the person responsible for that harm are likely to be at a similar point in terms of empathy: thinking of themselves and perceiving the other, if at all, as a source of threat to be feared and avoided. Their thought processes may almost mirror each other. Both are likely to hold the other in low regard. The person harmed may be perceived by their attacker as a nobody, or perhaps a lowlife who deserved what they got; those they harmed will often feel that their offender deserves whatever is coming to them – or worse. Some situations lead to aggression and even violence, which can stem from either side: the victim may be threatened or sought out and attacked to stop them 'grassing'; the offender may be hunted down for vengeance (although it should be pointed out that despite the murderous feelings commonly described by people harmed by crime, retaliation is rare).

Those harmed tend to blame themselves; those responsible to blame others – one directing blame inward; one directing it outwards. Either way, empathy and understanding are often quite naturally at rock bottom, at Empathy Level Zero (see Figure 2.3).

Figure 2.3: In terms of empathy for the other person, the person responsible and the person harmed mirror one another

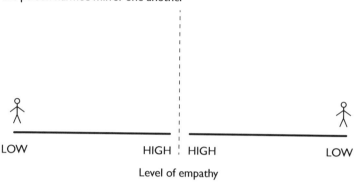

LOW   HIGH ⋮ HIGH   LOW

Level of empathy

If no one is caught

Comparing the total number of crimes that people surveyed say they have experienced with the number of crimes recorded by the police indicates that fewer than half of all crimes are reported – the so-called 'dark figure of crime' (see Figure 2.4).[11] There are several reasons why people don't report. They may not have realised that it was a crime, they may feel intimidated, they may not believe that it will be investigated or they may doubt that reporting it will make a difference. Perhaps they think it was too trivial and can't be bothered. Even if they do report, the person causing the harm is unlikely to get caught – clear-up rates for criminal investigations are about 28% (although this figure varies by crime type: for murder, the culprit is almost always caught, less important crimes such as shoplifting are more difficult to detect).[12] For most crimes, both parties are likely to remain at the bottom of the empathy

Figure 2.4: The dark figure of crime

Reported crime

The dark figure of crime

scale; the person who did it taking little or no responsibility, and the person they harmed left feeling aggrieved. Neither party has gained insight into the situation of the other, and there is zero opportunity for restoration or repair.

Some people who have been harmed who are denied or decline a restorative opportunity can simply 'forget' the offence. They may seem to be almost indifferent to what happened, recovering well and moving on rapidly with their lives. Even in areas with a well-established restorative justice service, at least half of those harmed by crime are likely to turn down the offer of restorative communication (Chapter Nine explores the take-up of restorative justice). Like those responsible, some block out their feelings – or take pleasure in thoughts of revenge, which eventually fade. The experience remains unresolved, and unless it was a serious offence, it gradually recedes into a nasty memory. It may change their character, leaving them more cautious, less trusting, more cynical and less adventurous than before, with bigger locks and alarms (both internal and external) to protect them against the world. Younger people may feel more inclined to go out and hurt others, and, as mentioned earlier, there is clear evidence that an early experience of victimisation can lead to future offending.[13]

Others do less well. They may be unable to get their tormentor out of their thoughts. A teenage boy was at home when a masked man broke in and attacked his father with a knife while he cowered behind the settee. For months afterwards, he was continuously ruminating on the event, a prisoner of the situation, unable to find release from that momentary entanglement of his life with that of the burglar. In his case, the person responsible was never caught and he couldn't opt for the potential release that might have come from a restorative process. He told his counsellor: "It is always there. It comes when I'm least expecting it."

In cases where the impact has been profound, without a resolution, the shadow of the experience is likely to continue to resurface, in some form or other, for example, through addictive behaviours, suicidal thoughts, feelings of shame and excessive self-blame, difficulties with relationships, dissociation (in which the individual becomes detached from reality), anxiety, and depression.[14] Physical injuries may eventually heal, but emotional scars can linger. And sometimes the body carries a constant reminder (a broken nose, a tooth that has to be removed, a scar covered by a scarf).

A grave crime can leave people trapped in fear, anger, guilt, blame and self-pity. Many are resilient and manage to find new ground, new meaning. For others, such a profound experience can blight lives and break spirits, casting a shadow that spoils everything and never lifts.

Meanwhile, the person responsible has learnt that if you get clean away with something, there are no consequences (for you). However, when challenged, most offenders acknowledge their wrongdoing and regret the harm they caused. Prisons are not full of people feeling proud to be known as a burglar, thief, sex offender, robber or murderer. Even if the actual act was intended and seemed like a good idea at the time, most, when encouraged to reflect, will recognise that it went too far – particularly if they are led into some insight into its consequences. They may block it out, but the harm they dealt is within them too. Denied an opportunity for repair and restoration, they become less inhibited and considerate, more callous and cocky – and statistically more likely to do it again. A life lesson about the cause and effect of their personal actions is lost, along with a crucial opportunity for developing empathy.

The gap

Crime separates people. In the hours, days and weeks following a crime, a gap is opened up between the person harmed and the person responsible (see Figure 2.5).

Figure 2.5: Both may start at the bottom of the empathy scale, with a large gap (social distance) between them

The person responsible		The person harmed
𝗑	**The gap**	𝗑
LOW		LOW

Level of empathy

If the people involved already knew one another, the crime may rip their relationship in two. If they were strangers, the connection created by the crime is immediately cut off – at least on a physical level. Psychologically, the incident is far from forgotten.

Many crimes are quite intimate – those of a violent or sexual nature usually involve intense proximity at the time of the offence. Others, for example, property crimes, are an invasion of privacy and a violation of personal space. However, in most criminal cases, there is little or no contact between the parties in the immediate aftermath. The person responsible is avoiding arrest, or has been apprehended and is in custody. The person harmed may be skirting around parts of their neighbourhood for fear of meeting their attacker. A colleague shared her experience of being burgled by someone who had done some casual gardening work for her. One day, she noticed that she had been avoiding town without being fully aware of doing so. She wasn't exactly scared of meeting the person who had burgled her, but somehow dreaded a chance meeting, which would involve an awkward exchange.

Some people drop out of education or employment following a crime. If the offence was serious, they may be frightened to go out at all; I have met a number of people who have become virtual prisoners in their own home.

If the crime is between people who already know each other, they may continue to see one another in their daily lives, but avoid communicating about the incident. Some people studiously evade eye contact and keep their heads lowered. This avoidance may be because they feel it will be less dangerous, because they aren't ready to face each other or because the police or lawyers are telling one or both parties to have no contact with the other while the offence is under investigation.

For whatever reason, a crime that starts with a connection – a relationship – and that leads to a serious breach of that relationship is followed by a gap. It is hard to have empathy for another person if you have no idea about what they are going through, and the gap is a powerful empathy suppressor.

They might as well be on different sides of a ravine, even if they share the same neighbourhood, classroom, household or even the same bed.

A graphic example of the gap that ensues even within a household involves a mother desperate to tell her son what it felt like for her when in a rage he threw her across the room, leaving her covered in bruises. She needed to explain to him that she continued to feel unsafe in her own home, and could never let down her guard when he was around. She was unable to have that conversation, to reach across the chasm, even while making his breakfast and sending him off to school. Sadly, a restorative process was not available in this case, and after repeated episodes of violence, she finally felt unable to manage. Her son was taken into care.

Cartoon 2.2: Crime creates a gap...

Cartoon 2.3: ...as if there was a ravine between people

Notes

[1.] Restorative Justice Council (2013) 'Kelvin's story', *Resolution*, Spring Newsletter, p 10.

[2.] Sykes, G. and Matza, D. (1957) 'Techniques of neutralization: a theory of delinquency', *American Sociological Review*, vol 22, no 6, pp 664–70. Similarly, Albert Bandura talked about 'mechanisms of moral disengagement', putting forward four mechanisms that enable people to selectively disengage their internal moral controls in order to perform 'reprehensible acts'. These are: reconstruing conduct; displacing or diffusing responsibility; disregarding or misrepresenting injurious consequences; and dehumanising or blaming the victim. Bandura, A. (1991) 'Social cognitive theory of moral thought and action', in W.M. Kurtines and J.L. Gewirtz (eds) *Handbook of moral behavior and development: Theory, research and applications* (vol A), Hillsdale, NJ: Erlbaum, pp 71–129.

[3.] Grossman, D. (1995) *On killing: The psychological cost of learning to kill in war and society*, New York, NY: Back Bay Books/Little Brown & Company.

[4.] Marshall, S. (1947) 'Men against fire: the problem of battle command in future war', *Infantry Journal*, Washington: Infantry Journal; New York, NY: William Morrow and co, c.1947.

[5.] Chambers, J. (2003) 'SLA Marshalls *Men against fire*: new evidence regarding fire ratios' (http://strategicstudiesinstitute.army.mil/pubs/parameters/articles/03autumn/chambers.pdf).

[6.] Grossman, D. (1995) *On killing: The psychological cost of learning to kill in war and society*, New York, NY: Back Bay Books/Little Brown & Company.

[7.] Sykes, G. and Matza, D. (1957) 'Techniques of neutralization: a theory of delinquency', *American Sociological Review*, vol 22, no 6, pp 664–70.

[8.] A trigger is 'where something or someone will remind the person of an aspect of the initial experience. This can lead to feelings of distress similar to those they felt at the time, which may be debilitating, for example fireworks triggering a startle response'. Wallis, P. (2010) *Are you okay? A practical guide to helping young victims of crime*, London: JKP, p 113.

[9.] Marian Partington, quoted in Cherry, S. (2012) *Healing agony*, London: Continuum Books, p 105. See also Partington, M. (2012) *If you sit very still*, Bristol: Vala Publishing. This is an extraordinary account by Marian Partington of her struggle with grief and rage after she learnt that her sister Lucy, who had been missing for 20 years had been kidnapped, tortured and killed by Fred and Rosemary West, and her determination to find a compassionate response and 'salvage the sacred'.

[10.] www.restorativejustice.org.uk/rj-in-action/ray_and_vi_donovan__meeting_our_sons_killer/

[11.] http://crime-study.blogspot.co.uk/2011/03/dark-figure-of-crime.html, The Open University, Milton Keynes. The Crime Survey for England and Wales (CSEW) estimated that there were 8.5 million crimes experienced by households and resident adults in the year ending June 2013. The police recorded 3.7 million offences over the same period; see Office for National Statistics (2013) 'Crime in England and Wales, year ending June 2013'(www.ons.gov.uk/ons/dcp171778_331209.pdf).

[12.] Of crimes recorded during 2008/09, 28% were cleared up by a sanction detection (where the person who committed the offence is brought to justice with a formal sanction). Walker, A., Flatley, J. and Mood, D. (eds) (2009) *Crime in England & Wales 2008/9, Home Office statistical bulletin 11/09, volume 1*, London: Home Office.

[13.] See, for example, McAra, L. and McVie, S. (2007) *Criminal justice transitions*, Edinburgh: University of Edinburgh; Owen, R. and Sweeting, A. (2007) 'Hoodie or goodie? The link between violent victimisation and offending in young people', prepared for Victim Support by BMRB Social Research (www.victimsupport.org.uk/~/media/Files/Publications/ResearchReports/hoodie-or-goodie-report.ashx).

[14.] See, for example, Rothschild, B. (2000) *The body remembers: The psychophysiology of trauma and trauma treatment*, New York, NY: W.W. Norton & Company.

Part Two
Empathy Level One: seeing

The conventional criminal justice system focuses upon three questions: (1) What laws have been broken? (2) Who did it? and (3) What do they deserve?

(Umbreit, Vos, Coates and Lightfoot, 2005)[1]

CHAPTER THREE

Entering the criminal justice system

Restorative justice is only possible in cases where someone is identified as the 'offender' and is caught. If no one is apprehended and the crime enters the records as 'no result', for those harmed, there is no formal acknowledgement, no chance to be 'seen', no opportunity for a 'hearing', no recognition of the harm they have suffered.[2] They are invisible. Without the criminal justice system, without the police, investigations, the Crown Prosecution Service (CPS) and the courts, there would be very little restorative justice.

Police investigation

If a crime is reported, witness statements are taken and an investigation is initiated. It can then take days or weeks before someone is apprehended and arrested. This can leave an awkward pause, when the person responsible may be wondering whether they have got away with it, and those harmed are waiting to find out if anyone will be arrested.

Sometimes, the person who caused the harm wishes to make amends, but doesn't know how, or fears that trying to could make things worse. Once they have been arrested, the criminal justice system may deliberately prohibit communication during the investigation. Both parties may be advised not to attempt contact with the other, or there may be bail conditions to keep people apart. Although put in place to protect those involved, these conditions can cause distress if they aren't clearly understood by everyone – and most people have no idea how the criminal justice system works. Some people harmed by crime say that in the hours and days following the incident, once they had been informed that someone was arrested, they started waiting for that person to come round to apologise. If the perpetrator is a young person, they can't understand why a parent hasn't marched him or her round immediately to say sorry.

In one case a girl was assaulted at her friend's party and someone who witnessed the attack called the police. When she learnt that a boy had been arrested, the girl's mother went round to his house to ask why he hadn't apologised. When the boy's father answered the door, she was too incensed to listen to what he was trying to explain – that

Cartoon 3.1: The police may discourage or forbid communication...

his son's bail conditions forbade any communication, direct or indirect. It almost came to blows.

Some cases lead to 'no further action' (NFA), usually because there is insufficient evidence or the complainant decides to withdraw the allegation: they may feel that simply calling the police about the offence has changed the situation; the person responsible may have made an emotional appeal for them to recant; or they may have been threatened or intimidated. Perhaps they now feel that a criminal justice response will be too heavy-handed, feel daunted by the court process or prefer to see whether the situation can be sorted out amicably.

Pure restorative justice

Sometimes (regardless of where the case gets to in the criminal justice system), the restorative encounter happens spontaneously – particularly when the people involved already know one another. Most restorative practitioners will have cases where by the time they start making contact with people, they are told that it has already been 'sorted'. This is good news (providing someone checks in with both parties to ensure that everyone concurs with this view). I would call this 'pure restorative justice', the ideal situation in which those involved repair the harm between them with no need for intervention from the professionals.

Cartoon 3.2: Job done!

Once someone has been arrested, they enter the criminal justice system.[3] They may be dealt with pre-court by the police through a fine (often called a fixed penalty notice), warning, conditional caution or caution if the offence is relatively minor. In fact, the fine is the most common outcome from the criminal justice system and therefore 'the most frequently used means of punishing, deterring, compensating and regulating throughout the legal system'.[4] Many fines are imposed for crimes that have no victim to compensate, such as for speeding or not wearing a seat belt. In those cases where people have been harmed, the fine is imposed without consulting the injured party or attempting to address their needs, and dispensed without any consideration for reparation, social connectedness or moral value.[5] This is the end of the road for restorative justice.

'On-the-spot' restorative justice

For minor offences, such as low-level anti-social behaviour, there is a lot of debate about 'on the spot' restorative approaches, which can be used as an alternative to an arrest. In some areas, the police are trained to deliver 'street' restorative justice interventions under initiatives designed to give them greater discretion. There are strong arguments for keeping minor cases out of the criminal justice system altogether, and there are situations when an instant response to sort out a crisis can work well. However, this is a challenging area of restorative practice, requiring considerable skill. Unfortunately, the restorative justice training provided to the police in some areas is minimal.

Pre-court restorative justice

Following an arrest, the police may offer the person responsible the option of a caution or other 'out-of-court disposal', which, if complied with, takes the place of a prosecution. For a caution to be administered, the perpetrator will have to accept his or her guilt. In the case of a conditional caution, the caution is given with 'conditions' that must be complied with, which could have one or more of the following objects: '(a) facilitating the rehabilitation of the offender; (b) ensuring that the offender makes reparation for the offence; and (c) punishing the offender'.[6] Failure to comply can lead to the perpetrator being prosecuted.

In some cases, a caution can include a provision for restorative justice. Many areas run successful 'diversion schemes', particularly for young people, where restorative justice forms part of a brief intervention programme aimed at addressing offending while keeping the person responsible out of court.

A more balanced system? The notion of 'parallel justice'

Restorative justice can often address the issues both leading up to and arising from lower-level crimes without recourse to court. A restorative meeting will explore creative ways to resolve the conflict, often resulting in an outcome agreement that satisfies the needs and wishes of all parties.

More serious crimes generate deeper needs. The model of 'parallel justice' acknowledges that both the person who has caused harm and the person harmed require 'justice' in its broadest sense.

There is an exercise that often forms part of restorative justice practitioner training[7] in which the trainees are given pieces of flipchart paper and invited to create two lists on the following topics: 'What do I need to feel better if I have been harmed?'; and 'What do I need to feel better if I have caused harm?' Each list is gradually filled with suggestions. Some are unique to one side or the other. If the person harmed was injured during the offence or lost out financially, they may need medical treatment or compensation. If the person responsible has a substance misuse or anger management problem, there may be specialist interventions that can help. There are other needs in common: trainees often identify things like respect, a listening ear, to be believed, safety, time and space to express difficult emotions, recognition, support, and so on. The two lists are compared and – lo and behold – it becomes clear that many of the needs of the person responsible and the person harmed are exactly the same.

In parallel justice, those needs are met separately for each party by a range of criminal justice, health, victim support and welfare services. The two sides run in parallel like two train tracks, each party receiving 'justice' to move them forwards (see Figure 3.1). If criminal justice agencies operated to this model, all their services would be made equally available to all their clients – those harmed in addition to those responsible for the harm – creating a more balanced and holistic response to crime. In reality, the weight of resources is overwhelmingly focused on those who cause harm, and there are serious gaps in victim services, particularly for young people.[8]

Figure 3.1: Parallel justice

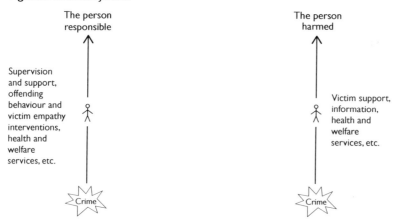

Some people on restorative justice training include the word 'punishment' on one or even both of the lists. They may argue that punishment provides a sense of vindication to the person harmed for the wrong that was done to them, and for the person who caused harm, it offers a way of passing through pain, taking the bitter medicine and coming out on the other side, where the harm they caused is formally dealt with and can be put behind them.

The training participants may also note that punishment is part of an agenda that goes beyond the needs of the parties directly involved in the offence. More serious or persistent offences bring another player into the conflict, with its own set of 'needs' – the state. I have never tried it, but it would be interesting to create a third list to identify what society needs in the aftermath of a serious offence.

Notes

[1] Umbreit, M.S., Vos, B., Coates, R.B. and Lightfoot, E. (2005) 'Restorative justice in the twenty first century: a social movement full of opportunities and pitfalls', *Marquette Law Review*, vol 89, no 2, pp 251–304, at p 258.

[2] Although having reported the crime, they may ask for help from Victim Support and may be eligible for Criminal Injuries Compensation – both of which are sources of support outside the criminal justice system.

[3] To simplify this account, entry into the criminal justice system is described as the point of arrest. There are a number of reasons why a person may be arrested, which are laid out in the Police and Criminal Evidence Act 1984 (PACE). Some of the common reasons for an arrest would be; to ensure that a potential suspect won't disappear off and become untraceable; to prevent them from causing criminal damage or injury to themselves or others; to ascertain their name and address, or; to allow for the prompt investigation of an offence or of their conduct. However, if these circumstances don't apply (for example if an arrest would be disproportionate) but the police wish to talk to someone in relation to an investigation, they may deem it unnecessary to arrest them, and the individual may instead be invited to attend a voluntary interview under caution. A third route into the criminal justice system would be if someone is reported for service of a summons direct to court, which would be most common for 'summary offences' such as a road traffic offence like speeding where the evidence is indisputable. All of these entries into the criminal justice system, with or without an arrest, could potentially progress to a pre-court disposal such as a caution or to prosecution.

[4] O'Malley, P. (2009) *The currency of justice: Fines and damages in consumer societies*, Abingdon: Routledge-Cavendish.

[5] If the case goes to court, the law says that compensation should take precedence over fines. By virtue of section 130 subsection 2A of the Criminal Justice Act 1982, the court must consider making a Compensation Order in any case where Section 130 empowers it to do so. The court is required to give reasons if it does not make a Compensation Order in a case where it is empowered to do so. Under section 130(12), if it would be appropriate both to impose a fine and to make a Compensation Order, but if the offender has insufficient means to pay both, the court has to give preference to compensation, although it may impose (a suitably reduced) fine as well.

[6.] Criminal Justice Act 2003, section 22(3).

[7.] This exercise remains uncredited as I haven't managed to establish who first introduced it into restorative justice training.

[8.] Oxfordshire has developed a unique service, called *SAFE!*, to support young people who have experienced crime. Some referrals to *SAFE!* are for young people who are in the criminal justice system already as perpetrators. Providing timely support by offering an empathetic ear for young people (based on a protective behaviours model) can help prevent future crime (www.safeproject.org.uk/).

CHAPTER FOUR

Into the criminal courts

If the offer of an 'out-of-court disposal' is refused, if any conditions attached to it are not complied with or if the offence is serious, the police can either make a decision to prosecute the person responsible themselves or refer the case to the Crown Prosecution Service to do so.[1] In mediaeval times, it was the person aggrieved who would prosecute, but these days, the state steps in to defuse feuds and to ensure justice, recognising that the individual does not have the resources to investigate and prosecute a crime that is committed against them.

The role of the criminal courts is, first, to determine guilt or innocence for this particular breach of the law and then to impose a penalty. The government defines the purpose of the courts on their official website as follows: 'to deliver justice for all, by convicting and punishing the guilty and helping them to stop offending, while protecting the innocent'.[2] The courts are the forum provided by the state where a fair trial may be held, guilt or innocence established, and punishment imposed on the guilty.

The primary concern for the Crown Prosecution Service under their code is to prosecute when it is in the public interest, and when there is greater than a 50% chance of a conviction. The Crown Prosecution Service acts for the state, not for the person harmed (as in Regina vs Smith, where Regina is the Crown rather than the aggrieved). Sometimes, when the 'victim' makes it clear that they will not assist in a prosecution, the Crown Prosecution Service will drop the case, although the decision not to prosecute is much more likely to be due to lack of evidence. A prosecution will still go ahead even in circumstances where it is clear that more harm than good will be done to the person harmed. An example would be a situation involving 'historic' sexual abuse, where living through the attempts by the defence to undermine their evidence in order to get their client off the charge may in some cases be as bad or perhaps worse for the person harmed than the abuse itself. Moreover if the defendant, having been found guilty decides to appeal, this can result in the case being tried more than once, which can add further re-victimisation by the criminal justice system. The criminal courts are not for or about the 'victim'. They were never intended to be. They are the state's response to the breach of a law and not that of the person affected by the crime. Working off the third sheet of flipchart paper mentioned on page 44, which could read; 'What does the state need if someone has caused serious harm?', the primary consideration is whether a prosecution serves the public interest – society – rather than a specific concern for the needs or wishes of the individual who was harmed.

While everyone has the right to a trial, most defendants plead guilty, and the court can proceed to sentencing. Because the agenda isn't about them, in many cases, the person harmed by the offence isn't alerted about the court date, and if they are, they may not be specifically invited to attend, although they will be told the sentencing outcome. Unfortunately, this can leave people feeling marginalised, like 'passive objects in someone else's effort at justice'.[3]

For those who plead 'not guilty', maintaining that they 'didn't do it', the UK has developed an adversarial system of justice in order to sieve out the 'innocent' from the 'guilty'. The starting point is always the 'presumption of innocence' and the prosecution must establish 'beyond reasonable doubt' that the defendant committed the crime by looking for proof of guilt. The court's task is to ensure a fair trial, and it is a cardinal principle in English law that it is better that 10 guilty people are acquitted than that one innocent person is convicted.[4]

During a trial, one advocate (a solicitor or barrister) representing the defence is pitted against another advocate (another solicitor or barrister) speaking for the prosecution. Each side will present evidence and cross-examine witnesses to buttress their own case or undermine that of the other side, and argue for a conviction or acquittal, respectively. The evidence provided by both sides is placed under scrutiny, and any victims or witnesses will therefore be questioned to see if their story stands up. At the end of the trial, it is the task of the magistrates or jury to come to an impartial judgement about whether the defendant's account is – or may be – true, in which case, he or she should be acquitted.

Not guilty: the end of the road for restorative justice

If the defendant is found 'not guilty' and acquitted, or if the case fails in court, it is the end of the road for any formal restorative resolution. Most services will also automatically discount restorative justice as an option if a defendant pleads 'not guilty' and is found guilty at trial on the grounds that the defendant doesn't accept their part in what happened (although if they did meet, those harmed may find answers that are better than nothing – even from someone who will only admit to 'being there'). In these cases where restorative justice is not on the table, the criminal justice outcome is the only outcome available. The sentence handed down for someone found guilty at trial often brings some measure of relief to those harmed, knowing that 'something has been done', although many of the needs on their flipchart paper (see page 44) may be left unmet.

The focus of the criminal courts is predominantly on the defendant. Beyond providing evidence that may lead to a conviction, those harmed by the crime are by and large sidelined in the court process. The system is not designed or intended as a tool for facilitating communication between people who are in conflict; nor is it geared to addressing the impact of the crime on the wider circle of people who have been affected.

Some argue that the court experience does however have some 'quasi-restorative' aspects.[5] People who are harmed by a crime often express a need to be 'seen'; to be acknowledged as a central and ongoing part of the story of 'their' crime. If someone is brought before the court, the formality and ritual of the courtroom may help them feel that their matter is being taken seriously.

In cases involving a trial, it is common for the person responsible and the person harmed to be together in the same room, in close proximity for what is often only the second time (the first time being the offence itself). For some crimes it may be their first sighting of each other; in all cases it is a chance to see the other person in a different context. Literally clapping eyes on one another can sometimes help. The person responsible may show a more reflective side; if they were drunk during the offence, they will almost certainly be sober in court.

It is possible that this contact can help to close the gap caused by the crime, raising levels of empathy by allowing each side at least to be seen by the other, even if they are not allowed to communicate directly. In some cases it can help people make the first step towards a restorative journey.

If there is a trial, the court will listen to the accounts of all the parties, and the evidence that is put before the court may help fulfil people's need for information. An elderly woman who had been assaulted by a young man attended court as a witness. On hearing details about the lifetime of abuse suffered by the person who had attacked her, she said triumphantly: "I knew it! I'm not the victim – he is." The person harmed may be invited to make a Victim Personal Statement, which is a record of the personal impact of the crime, giving them 'a voice in the criminal justice process'.[6] They can read it aloud themselves or have it read aloud for them, usually by the prosecutor. Seeing closed-circuit television (CCTV) footage of an incident or pictures of injuries can help those harmed to feel vindicated, while the wrongdoer is often shocked to be reminded of what they did.

For the person who caused harm, the probation or youth offending service conducts a careful assessment of what went wrong, so that the sentence imposed can include programmes providing support to address their offence-related needs. When the sentence is passed, while it is debatable whether people learn much from punishment alone (except as a reminder to avoid being caught in future), there may be an opportunity to reflect on and atone for their actions through other elements of the court order, such as community service, reparation, victim empathy courses or other programmes in the community or custody.[7]

Financial compensation awarded by the court is another attempt at a potentially restorative outcome. Compensation creates a measure of restoration from the person responsible to the person harmed, based upon an assessment of the damage caused and the perpetrator's ability to pay. This can help the person harmed to feel that there is an element of accountability for those who hurt them (although, conversely, it can feel insulting if only a small amount is stipulated, and if paid in dribs and drabs, could be taken as proof that the perpetrator doesn't care, even if that isn't an intended message).

Finally, the sentencing remarks of the magistrates or judge can contain a helpful and often wise message. It will usually include a clear acknowledgement that the offence was wrong, that it has been taken seriously and that the harmful behaviour is condemned. Even though the court solution is imposed rather than negotiated, the criminal justice system reaches an outcome via the court's judgement that can provide some level of satisfaction and closure for those harmed, and start to close the gap (see Figure 4.1).

Unfortunately, when viewed through a restorative justice lens, the criminal justice response to crime can seem destructive.[8] This may well be inevitable in a forum for establishing guilt or innocence and passing sentence. Instead of closing the gap, it can act like a crowbar, intentionally or unintentionally enlarging it, further separating those involved in a crime by restricting communication and polarising their views.

For either side, seeing the other person in a courtroom context may not provide the best insight into that person's attitude, or the impact that the crime has had on them. The situation in court is highly charged, with everyone entrenching their positions as they hope for the 'best' outcome (for themselves). Each party will be surrounded by family and supporters, and the defendant, who is hoping for leniency, may

Figure 4.1: The criminal justice system can lift people up the empathy scale and start to close the gap between them

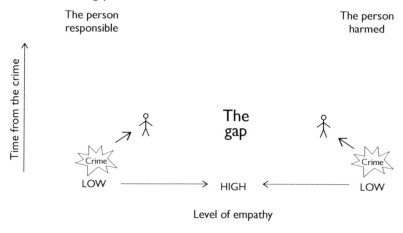

have their head bowed, having been instructed not to communicate with or approach the person they harmed. They may come across as glowering, or cocky and unremorseful. In this tense atmosphere, it is unlikely that the parties will really 'see' one another, and if their eyes do meet, they may misinterpret what is behind their expression, as Anaïs Nin pointed out: 'We do not see things as they are. We see things as we are'.[9] Stereotypes may remain unchallenged, and the person responsible is unlikely to understand the human consequences of their actions. Any direct contact is unlikely to be healing – especially if people meet in an inappropriate way, for example, in the court waiting area or canteen. Confrontations in court between the defendant and accuser may also increase animosity enormously.

Restorative justice works through the power of storytelling and narrative, the sharing of different perspectives on the same incident of harm. In restorative justice, what is important is what the participants find important. The criminal court has a very different purpose and focus, and is not designed to enhance communication or bring the parties closer. The defendant may be advised not to speak for themselves, and if they do speak, they will be restricted in how they tell their story. Their thoughts and feelings will be of minimal interest. If there is a trial, those who were affected by or witnessed the offence can have their 'day in court', but rather than being invited to share their story in the way they might wish to, they are likely to be grilled for information in the form of closed questions[10] that can break down any attempt that they might make to create a coherent narrative. They will be expected to revisit intimate details of the offence, to relive their pain, but will be denied any opportunity to ask questions of the accused (or the accused to answer them). Kim Book, whose daughter Nicole was murdered and who went on to become Executive Director of Victim Voices Heard, a restorative justice service in Delaware (see p xii) wrote:

> The judge and court did not kill Nicole; the young man sitting next to me killed her. Shouldn't I have the right to speak to him? Shouldn't he hear from me, since it was my life that he has changed?[11]

Conversely, while designed to give a voice to those hurt, if a Victim Personal Statement is read out in court it can become 'one-way emotional traffic without the safeguards brought about by deliberation'.[12]

With the prosecution seeking to secure a conviction, and the defence aiming to win their case – or at least helping their client to get off as lightly as possible – defendants are encouraged to fight for their innocence or give reasons to mitigate their punishment if they plead guilty. They may be persuaded into a guilty plea for actions they don't feel responsible for on the advice that it will lead to a lighter sentence than the one they might receive should they be found guilty after a trial. Meanwhile an informal 'deal' may be struck between defense lawyers and prosecutors, where, for example, the prosecution will drop a more serious charge(for example assault) in return for a guilty plea to a lesser charge (such as a public order offence). While this may be the only way that a conviction can be secured, witnessing their case being down-graded can leave the person harmed feeling doubted and re-victimised, that their experience has been discounted.

We've seen that with some crimes, it is fairly straightforward to distinguish between a guilty 'offender' and innocent 'victim', while others are more messy, with at least some degree of shared responsibility. Life, in all its complexity, also appears in court. During a trial, the jury have to unravel it all, to determine whether the defendant is guilty as charged despite the shades of grey. In some trials, it can become obvious to the court that the 'victim' and 'defendant' should be swapped. If a defendant is found guilty, the outcome from court almost inevitably reduces a complex situation down to a guilty 'offender' and innocent 'victim', which can create challenges down the line for the restorative practitioner.

Finally, a defendant may ask the court passing sentence to take other crimes of a similar nature into consideration (TIC) during sentencing. This allows them to 'clear the slate', as they avoid the risk of subsequent

Cartoon 4.1: A little bit innocent

prosecution for those offences. These cases can sometimes fall under the radar of a restorative service, as offences TIC may have less status than those where there has been a charge, and information may be scant. When Sari Stacey received a letter from the police to the effect that her burglary offence was one of 62 TICs she wasn't able to write a Victim Personal Statement and had to go through an arduous process before her request for a restorative meeting with the person who committed the offence was realised.[13]

While people's experience of court varies, from the perspective of those involved in the role of victim and witness, it is mostly positive despite its flaws. Many of the negative side effects of the criminal courts can be alleviated by keeping people informed and ensuring that they know what they can expect. High on the list of needs for people harmed by crime is information. Having lost control during the offence, they are now hungry for information in order to alleviate any uncertainty, wanting to know exactly what is happening in the aftermath of their bad experience. This need is recognised in the Victim's Code of Practice, which spells out the duties of the various criminal justice agencies, and those harmed should receive regular updates on their case from the police or witness services.[14]

Extreme cases where people are re-victimised in court occasionally hit the news, as was the case for Frances Andrade, a violin teacher who tragically killed herself after testifying against her old music teacher who'd committed sexual crimes. Having been told by the defendant's barrister that she was telling a 'pack of lies', she texted a friend three days before committing suicide to say she felt like she had been 'raped all over again' in the witness box. A recent report found that being 'aggressively cross examined' causes some people distress,[15] in recognition of which the revised Victims Code of Practice places a duty on the Crown Prosecution Service to 'treat victims who are witnesses in court respectfully and, where appropriate, seek the court's intervention where cross-examination is considered by the prosecutor to be inappropriate or too aggressive'.[16] The Code also sets out enhanced entitlements for victims of the most serious crimes, persistently targeted victims and those who are vulnerable or intimidated, and it is increasingly common for 'special measures' to be used, which mean that the witness/victim can give evidence via video link or behind screens. For child witnesses, these measures are automatically used.[17]

Victims and witnesses acknowledge the adversarial nature of the system, and Ministry of Justice surveys of adult victims' and witnesses' experiences indicate that the majority of people who go to court are satisfied with their contact with the criminal justice system and would be willing to engage with it again in future.[18] Most find that their needs are met, are happy that their experience has been taken seriously and dealt with, and, crucially, feel gratified that they have been believed. Many favour the formal court process and decline an invitation for restorative justice.

Crime and punishment

Once someone has either pleaded or been found guilty, the magistrates or judge pass sentence. The UK is a highly punitive nation. In 2011, Francis Cook, Chief Executive of the Howard League for Penal Reform, made the striking claim that: "We in this country have more life sentence prisoners than all of the other countries in the Council of Europe added together"[19] (there are 47 countries in the Council of Europe). Accepting that the aim of some custodial sentences can be to protect the public, many people who are locked up don't pose a risk to public safety. The increasingly punitive nature of penal policy can be attributed to the banging drums of the media and government paranoia rather than the particular desires of the judiciary. We are all fascinated by crime, and the media capitalises on this by the high profile given to lurid crime stories, spreading a false perception among the public that crime is out of control and rising, and leading to pressure on the political parties to call for ever-more punitive measures.[20]

For the defendant, a sentence passed down from court can cause stigma and rejection, and jeopardise their future; particularly if it involves a term in custody. Rather than rehabilitate their offending behaviour, let alone help them find healing, a prison sentence can serve to stamp 'criminal' onto someone's life story, often in permanent ink. 'In the eyes of society, a period of imprisonment serves to establish criminality as "an indelibly ontological attribute."' [21] Having entered the criminal justice system, it can become very hard to find the exit; almost two thirds of prisoners serving a sentence of less than 12 months reoffend and are back in prison within a year.[22]

Pointing an accusing finger at an individual's unacceptable behaviour allows society to label and punish large sections of the poor, minority groups, the young, the socially rebellious, the working class, the homeless, the mentally ill and those on benefits. It reinforces social divisions and lets the rest of us off the hook:

> We love to consume other people's troubles and embarrassments, and this makes sense because hearing about other people's problems makes us feel better about our own. Since we do not know these people, we live vicariously and judge them with no strings attached. We become armchair quarterbacks – deciding what people ought to do or ought not to have done. It is common for people to attach blame to strangers – this helps to reinforce the sense that we are not as vulnerable as they are because we are not like them; we would not make similar choices. Believing that we are different, or wiser, provides us with the illusion that we have some control over our own lives.[23]

Locking people up in prison also creates the largest and most physical gap between those directly involved in a crime – and with the community and wider society, too. Punishing someone for their wrongdoing may cause them to reflect, but carries a danger that it makes them feel that *they* are the 'victim' because the court is inflicting harm on *them*. Punishment, by encouraging the person responsible to think of self, not others, may inadvertently knock them further down the empathy scale – particularly if they blame their victim for getting them in trouble. Preoccupied with the consequences for themselves, they may not see beyond their own suffering to consider the consequences for those they have harmed. I recall a young man who had been convicted for a street robbery talking about his time when he had first arrived in prison on remand. At 2am or 3am, when everyone was shut in their cells and sleeping, when things finally quietened down, he would lie on his bed with the window open, listening to the wind. He would have visions of all the crimes that he had committed, thinking of ways he could have avoided getting caught, planning how to do it better next time. He would think about his family, and the pressure that his prison sentence would put them under. He would also think about the woman he had robbed. He said that he felt "pissed off" with her, thinking "this woman put me on remand", and "I'm really going to seriously hurt this woman when I get out." He had no idea that the woman he had robbed had quit college, was too scared to leave her home, just wanted to lock herself away and hide. It wasn't until he was given a custodial sentence and attended a victim empathy course in prison that he started to think about how she might be feeling about his release. His rage abated, and he agreed to a restorative meeting in order to offer his reassurance that she wouldn't be targeted again.

Retributive versus restorative

Some sociologists argue that the criminal justice process itself inflicts harm on those people who travel through the system, and that those harms may exceed the original harm caused by the crime.[24] There has been a tendency in restorative justice circles to draw a sharp distinction between 'retributive' and 'restorative', and it has been argued that there is a fundamental and irreconcilable difference between the value base of restorative justice, which they see as voluntary and empowering, putting people back in control of their lives, and criminal justice, whose processes are described as 'inherently coercive',[25] being based upon compulsion, disempowerment and the removal of control and choice.

Howard Zehr is considered one of the pioneers of restorative justice, and in his early writing, he asserted that criminal justice doesn't work either for those responsible or those harmed by crime, because it discourages 'real' offender accountability, while failing to take into account the needs of crime victims by defining crime as an offence against the state. Zehr created charts contrasting the two systems, and criminal justice and restorative justice were deemed to be pulling in opposite directions. Restorative justice was put forward as an alternative vision for justice.[26]

More recently, Zehr's view has changed, recognising that there is a public as well as a private dimension to crime:

I have come to believe that this polarization may be somewhat misleading.... There are larger concerns and obligations that belong to society beyond those who have a direct stake in a particular event. These include a society's concern for the safety, human rights, and the general well-being of its members. Many argue that the government has an important and legitimate role in looking after such societal concerns.[27]

How could the criminal justice system be more restorative?

Restorative justice, rather than replacing it, relies on the criminal justice system. In the aftermath of the offence, when they are trying to get away with it, restorative justice needs the person responsible to be caught. If that person is maintaining their innocence, the criminal court process is there to establish whether they are culpable.

When their empathy for those they harmed is low, an element of compulsion is required to get the perpetrator to the point when they will engage and start taking responsibility. Having reached this point, for minor crimes, it is often appropriate to divert the case from the criminal justice system, as we have seen, to explore whether the matter can be resolved to everyone's satisfaction and go down a purely restorative route.

For more serious crimes, few would consider a restorative process alone to be adequate. Through the criminal justice system, the state needs to step in to fulfil its 'obligations' and protect its citizens. It does this by addressing risk and considering the 'public interest', seeking to halt the offending behaviour and reassert the rules both for the person causing harm and as a message to wider society. Serious crimes are a major violation of the nation's rules – a rip in the social fabric – and the state must respond. A grave event demands a grave response, and the solemnity and ritual of a courtroom followed by a robust sentence underlines its disapproval and provides that *gravitas*.

A purely restorative process isn't adequate to address these wider needs. However, as we've seen, the court process alone does not adequately resolve the restorative needs of the parties involved in a crime. Most of the people on restorative justice training courses, including those with a punitive bent, accept that punishment cannot meet the majority of the needs on the two flipchart lists mentioned on page 44, and particularly those needs that may be unique to one party or the other: an explanation, an apology, a chance to say sorry, reassurance that it won't happen again. Some people harmed by crime, even if they initially embrace punishment, may ultimately find that simply hearing about the punishment of 'their' offender is not enough for them to recover. Some needs can *only* be met through communication.

Ideally, at some points along their parallel journeys, appropriate communication can therefore be facilitated between the person responsible and the person harmed, through a restorative process – like the rungs of a ladder – to facilitate understanding, repair and healing (see Figure 4.2). The question now becomes: 'Where does restorative justice fit in the criminal justice system?'

Figure 4.2: Parallel justice with restorative communication between the two parties

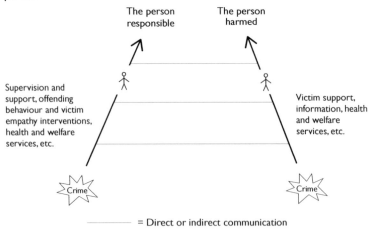

In the UK, there have been attempts to incorporate a restorative justice process into criminal justice at various points, most notably, in youth justice. In England and Wales the Youth Justice and Criminal Evidence Act 1999 introduced the Referral Order, which marked a significant move away from formal court processes towards a model of community-based sentencing.[28] When it came in, the Referral Order was the only mandatory form of youth sentence. The court had to impose a Referral Order if the following requirements were met: that the young person was aged 10–17; that they had not previously been convicted; that they were pleading guilty to the offence; and if the court was not considering an absolute or conditional discharge or imprisonment. Subsequent legislation has introduced the Youth Rehabilitation Order which can also be given to a young person in court for the first time, and removed the restriction on repeated use of the Referral Order, which remains the most common community sentence in youth justice. The 'referral' relates to the court referring a young person who has pleaded guilty to a special panel, which is convened by volunteer representatives of the community. The panel is a restorative meeting, to which the person harmed is invited, along with the young person's parents, supporters for both parties and significant others. During the meeting, a programme of interventions is negotiated to repair the harm caused by the offence and address the unmet needs that led to the crime being committed by the young person. Once the programme is agreed, it is written up as a contract that becomes legally binding, so that the young person can be returned to court if they don't comply.

New Zealand has a similar process, in which restorative justice is embedded in the court system for young people who offend. Under the Children Young Persons & Their Families Act 1989, a restorative process called a 'family group conference' (FGC) operates within the legal framework of the youth justice system for all medium and serious cases, except murder and manslaughter.[29] If a young person is in the youth court charged with an offence, the court adjourns for an FGC involving the young person and their family, those harmed by the crime, and other parties with a stake in the offence. In common with a Referral Order, everyone shares their perspective of what happened and joins in negotiating a plan for the young person to address the harm caused by the crime and keep them out of trouble in future. There is no legislative prescription for FGC plans, which allows for creative and individually tailored resolutions. Because the plan has been created and is owned by those with a stake in the offence, it is likely to be appropriate, achievable and based on the resources and support of the family and their community. Once the plan is agreed, it is put back before the court, which will check that it is practicable, and, crucially, that it is proportionate in comparison with the outcomes from other cases involving similar offences. The court thus retains a role in supervising and monitoring the plans. In the first four years following their introduction, 18 institutions for youth who offended were closed and the country has seen a 54% decrease in the number of young people being transferred up to the adult jurisdiction (transfer to the adult system is usually for a prison sentence). The use of FGCs is mandatory and there are currently approximately 7,000 each year.[30]

When, in 2001, Northern Ireland adopted a similar model of restorative conferencing orders for young people based upon the New Zealand model, it also resulted in a dramatic reduction in custodial sentences, to a third the level found in the rest of the UK. Restorative justice now seems set to move closer to the heart of the court process

—

across the UK, and the British government is paying close attention to lessons that can be learned from both New Zealand and Northern Ireland. The Crime and Courts Act 2013 allows for the youth and adult courts to defer a case for up to six months for a restorative process to be explored before sentencing for any case coming through court. Although the court still retains its role in deciding the sentence, it could potentially incorporate elements from a restorative justice agreement into the sentence and the court will decide, in accordance with Sentencing Guidelines, if any weight is to be given to the defendant's participation in the restorative meeting. In common with Northern Ireland and New Zealand, youth custody levels in England and Wales are dropping significantly, with many units decommissioned as a result.

Each of the models for incorporating restorative justice mentioned here have their strengths and weaknesses. There is an inherent danger in linking restorative justice to sentencing, which can lead the person responsible to feign remorse in order to benefit from their involvement. Most people harmed who engage in restorative justice are keen to know that involvement in the process won't reduce the rest of the perpetrator's sentence. There are also sensitivities around inviting the person harmed to a restorative meeting to fit in with the perpetrator's criminal justice process. A colleague who was invited to attend a Referral Order panel for a young person who burgled her house told me:

> "The overall tone of the letter I received (including the specific reference to it as the young offender's meeting) implied that it wasn't for or about my needs as the victim of the crime, and that I was an optional extra. Whose meeting was it? – clearly not mine. My own view is that a lot of victims choose not to participate in panel meetings at present because they are protecting themselves from a process that they sense from the start isn't truly about them or their needs."

Since their introduction, Referral Orders have had a disappointingly low level of involvement from those harmed, although this varies widely across England and Wales. This situation has led to a requirement for all Youth Offending Team workers and volunteers to be trained in restorative justice facilitation in order to improve the quality and consistency of restorative skills in panels, and support improved engagement by those harmed during the process. Putting their needs on an equal footing to the person responsible is part of the challenge of using restorative justice within a criminal justice system.

Court-imposed timescales can also be an issue. In New Zealand, there is a seven-day time frame for convening a Court-directed FGC.[31] The legal definition for 'convened' means that the date, time and venue has been set in consultation with the person responsible, their family, those harmed and the enforcement officer. The FGC must then be completed within seven days of being convened unless there are special reasons (eg the readiness of professional reports or the availability of the people harmed or key family members). This timescale can create a tension between building a rapport with those harmed by the offence and meeting the requirements of the legislation.

The jury is out on where restorative justice best sits in criminal justice: before sentencing, after sentencing or as an alternative to a court-imposed sentence. Restorative justice is still in its early days, and the Referral Order, Family Group Conference and Restorative Conferencing Order are brave and inspiring attempts to turn criminal justice inside out, transferring decision making from the court to the community, from people with no stake in the offence to those who were directly involved. Wherever it ends up sitting, in addition to addressing the flipchart needs of the person responsible and person harmed, restorative justice can help the criminal justice system. With less than half of all crimes being reported, the criminal justice system needs people to be satisfied with their experience and pleased to come forward as witnesses in the future. Direct restorative justice typically returns satisfaction figures for people harmed by crime of 85% or more, with randomised trials showing that 'victims [who attend a restorative meeting] are far more satisfied than their counterparts whose cases are dealt with by the criminal justice process'.[32] Restorative justice also delivers promising reductions in offending. Professor Lawrence Sherman and Dr Heather Strang have carried out research which indicates that restorative justice can reduce the frequency of reoffending by 27% – 'that is 27% less crime and 27% fewer people harmed by crime'.[33]

More fundamentally, restorative justice helps to move those harmed by crime from the margins of the criminal justice system to centre stage:

> No longer bit-part players in too many mysterious court hearings, reduced to the status of witnesses, heard and then forgotten, victims find themselves consulted and involved in a brand new process of making amends ... a dignified role in resolution.[34]

We've seen that for more serious cases, a restorative process alone, no matter how powerful, is insufficient to address the depth and gravity of the offence and its consequences. Some people are too dangerous to be allowed to walk free; some crimes have repercussions that can't be addressed simply though a restorative meeting. Victims' Voices Heard, an American restorative justice programme working with the most serious cases, operates at the end of the criminal justice process, often many years after sentencing. In their experience, 'the victims ... felt strongly that their offenders needed to be held accountable by the criminal justice system. They did not wish to side-step that aspect of justice and punishment.'[35] In serious cases, both a criminal justice and restorative process work together. Pitching one against the other creates a false dichotomy.

Notes

[1] The police can prosecute cases, although a case will be referred to the Crown Prosecution Service if the offence is indictable only, if it is an 'either way' offence for which a 'not guilty' plea is anticipated, or if it would not be suitable for summary trial.

[2] www.cjsonline.gov.uk

[3] From an Opinion article by Macdonald, K. (2010) 'Stop dumping children in warehouse prisons', *The Times*, 15 July, p 21.

[4] The phrase 'It is better that ten guilty escape than one innocent suffer' is attributed to the jurist Sir William Blackstone in 1765; see *Commentaries on the Laws of England Books 1–4 (1765–1769)* Commentary 358 (www.lonang.com/exlibris/blackstone/bla-000.htm).

[5] Caroline Hoyle makes this argument in Cunneen, C. and Hoyle, C. (2010) *Debating restorative justice*, Oxford: Hart.

[6] Code of Practice for Victims of Crime (2013) section 1.11. The Criminal Practice Direction (Sentencing) guidelines state that when a police officer takes a statement, the victim *should* be told about the option of making a Victim Personal Statement, and says the court *will* take the statement into account at sentencing stage (www.gov.uk/government/uploads/system/uploads/attachment_data/file/254459/code-of-practice-victims-of-crime.pdf).

[7] The Howard League for Penal Reform points out that reconviction rates for those serving community sentences are 14% lower than for those serving

time in jail, at a fraction of the cost (www.howardleague.org/fileadmin/howard_league/user/pdf/Community_sentences_factsheet.pdf).

[8.] Howard Zehr introduced the analogy of lenses: Zehr, H. (1990) *Changing lenses – a new focus for crime and justice*, Harrisonburg, VA: Herald Press.

[9.] Nin, A. (1961) *Seduction of the Minotaur*, Chicago, IL: Swallow Press, p 124.

[10.] Closed questions are questions that can only be answered with a 'yes' or 'no', or require a simple factual answer, for example, 'Is your name John Smith?' or 'How old are you?'

[11.] Miller, S. (2011) *After the crime*, New York, NY: New York University Press, p 29.

[12.] Cunneen, C. and Hoyle, C. (2010) *Debating restorative justice*, Oxford: Hart, p 64.

[13.] Lummer, R., Nahrwold, M. and Süß, B. (eds) (2012) *Restorative justice – a victim perspective and issues of co-operation*, Keil: Fachhochschule, p 129. Thames Valley Restorative Justice Service now has a European-funded, 'victim-led' project specifically geared for people harmed by crime to access restorative justice.

[14.] *Code of practice for victims of crime* is available at: www.gov.uk/government/uploads/system/uploads/attachment_data/file/254459/code-of-practice-victims-of-crime.pdf

[15.] Hunter, G., Jacobson, J. and Kirby, A. (2013) *Out of the shadows, victims' and witnesses' experiences of attending the Crown Court*, London: Institute for Criminal Policy Research, University of London, p 34.

[16.] *Code of practice for victims of crime* (2013) Ministry of Justice, London: The Stationery Office, paragraph 3.2.

[17.] Code of Practice for Victims of Crime (2013) sections 1.1 and 3.3, respectively.

[18.] Franklyn, R. (2012) *Satisfaction and willingness to engage with the Criminal Justice System, Findings from the Witness and Victim Experience Survey, 2009–10*, London: Ministry of Justice. These surveys involved approximately 35,000 telephone interviews with adult victims and prosecution witnesses in England and Wales and were conducted annually until 2011.

[19.] Frances Cook, Chief executive of the Howard League for Penal Reform, speaking on the *Today* programme, 27 October 2011.

[20.] Sara Beale makes this argument, see Beale, S. (2006) 'The news media's influence on criminal justice policy: how market-driven news promotes punitiveness', *William and Mary Law Review*, Volume 48, Issue 2, Article 2, pp 396–476 (http://scholarship.law.wm.edu/wmlr/).

[21.] Marshall, C. (2001) *Beyond retribution*, Cambridge: WM B Erdmanns Publications, p 117, quoting Cayley, D. (1998) *The expanding prison*, Toronto: House of Anansi Press Limited, p 41.

[22.] open.justice.gov.uk/reoffending/prisons/

[23.] Miller, S. (2011) *After the crime*, New York, NY: New York University Press, p 3.

[24.] See, for example, Hillyard, P., Pantazis, C., Gordon, D. and Tombs, S. (eds) (2004) *Beyond criminology; taking harm seriously*, London: Pluto Press.

[25.] Sanders, A. and Young, R. (2007) *Criminal justice* (3rd edn), Oxford: Oxford University Press. Some authors argue that there are also coercive elements in restorative justice, a theme that is explored in Chapter Eight.

[26.] Zehr, H. (1985) 'Retributive justice, restorative justice', *New perspectives on crime and justice* (Issue #4), Akron, PA: Mennonite Central Committee Office of Criminal Justice.

[27.] Zehr, H. (2002) *The little book of restorative justice*, Intercourse, PA: Good Books.

[28.] Referral Orders are now made under sections 16–18 of the Powers of Criminal Courts Sentencing Act 2000, which consolidated a number of other Acts. The Referral Order has been strengthened by the Legal Aid, Sentencing and Punishment of Offenders Act 2012, which removed the restriction on repeated use of the Referral Order.

[29.] Morris, A. and Gabrielle, M. (1998) 'Restorative justice in New Zealand: family group conferences as a case study', *Western Criminology Review*, vol 1, no 1 (http://wcr.sonoma.edu/v1n1/index.html).

[30.] These figures were quoted by Allan MaCrae, Youth Justice Regional Advisor (South), New Zealand, during a presentation to the 'Restoring the Balance' Conference at St Catherine's College, Oxford, on 28 November 2013 (www.thamesvalleypartnership.org.uk/ccc/resources/past-events?ccc=restorative-justice).

[31.] Time limits for the convening of family group conferences are outlined in sections 249(c) and 249(6) of the Children, Young Persons, and Their Families Act 1989: substituted, on 8 January 1995, by section 35 of the Children, Young Persons, and Their Families Amendment Act 1994 (1994 No 121).

[32.] Heather Strang, University of Cambridge, from a presentation to the Restoring the Balance conference at St Catherine's College, Oxford, on 28 November 2013, entitled 'Victims and restorative justice: what do we know from international research evidence?'

[33.] Shapland, J., Robinson, G. and Sorsby, A. (2011) *Restorative justice in practice*, London: Routledge. The Restorative Justice Council regularly produces updates on current research into the efficacy of restorative justice, including its impact on recidivism. Restorative justice is one of the most heavily researched fields in criminal justice (www.restorativejustice.org.uk/restorative_justice_works/).

[34.] From an Opinion article by Macdonald, K. (2010) 'Stop dumping children in warehouse prisons', *The Times*, 15 July, p 21.

[35.] Miller, S. (2011) *After the crime*, New York, NY: New York University Press, p 12.

—

Part Three
Empathy Level Two: voicing

We look for repair, and in that repair, we cause no further harm.

(Restorative justice maxim, source unknown)

CHAPTER FIVE

Unripe restorative justice

Pacing and timing

One of the trickiest aspects of successful restorative justice involves getting the timing right for participants, within the constraints of the criminal justice system's own process from arrest through to conviction and sentence. Having entered the criminal justice system, the conflict is dealt with at the system's pace, which can take anything from a few days for a caution to be delivered to months or even years for a complex trial to progress through to sentence. By the time the person who caused harm has met potentially dozens of professionals and gone through a range of criminal justice hoops, any initial empathy and remorse that existed may have faded.

Trials and sentencing for serious offences involve a long drawn-out process, which can leave everyone frozen in anticipation of the next stage in an endless series of dates, with little chance for moving on or finding closure. Each point on the long journey can open the wound for those harmed, who are forced to continually revisit the original trauma in a way that is not healing. Even if the person responsible does end up in prison, they may appeal against conviction or sentence, and as their sentence progresses, they can eventually request early release. These applications for leniency may be simply a formality for the perpetrator but can be perceived as a lack of remorse or unwillingness to accept responsibility for those harmed. Having finally breathed a sigh of relief when their tormentor was safely locked away, those harmed may find themselves unable to start grieving until the final date – which may not come until the perpetrator's licence (the period of statutory supervision back in the community) is completed – while for some, this too can bring fresh anxieties.

If the harmed party is invited into a restorative process months or years down the line, they may say that they have put the incident behind them, that it is already sorted or that they don't want to reopen old wounds. For some, though, it helps if a period of time is allowed to elapse before a restorative meeting. One woman who had been burgled chose to wait until the young man who burgled her had completed all of the requirements of his community order before agreeing to meet him. She felt that this would give him a chance to demonstrate that he was truly sorry through his actions.

For more serious crimes, the delay can be appropriate; it will be too early for a restorative resolution, for an instant apology or instant forgiveness (forgiveness is discussed in Chapter Thirteen). Either sentiment may be expressed, but as both apology and forgiveness are a path and a process rather than a quick-fix solution, they may not be timely. The apology or forgiveness will not be informed by insight into the other 'story' and therefore not fully restorative.

Cartoon 5.1: So sorry...

Perhaps a more natural response is that of Vi Donovan. When she heard that her son, Chris, had been murdered, her immediate reaction was to run out of the door, to find her son's killers and to "do to them what they had done to Chris". For Vi and her husband Ray, it took 10 years to reach the point when they were both able to say "we forgive you" to the young men who murdered Chris.[1] Each situation is unique, and the built-in delay before any restorative justice process starts can either be a help or a hindrance.

Positional stalemate

As the initial shock of the incident subsides, everyone involved in the crime may start to settle into positions. To make sense of what happened, to retain their own sense of worth following what is often a shameful experience, they may form opinions and a storyline about the offence, about themselves, about their situation and about the other. If one or both parties remain low down on the empathy scale, those positions may be based upon a sense of grievance about the other and can become more fixed as time passes.

The restorative practitioner knows that the most powerful way for those fixed positions to change, to challenge denial, to allow for empathy to develop, is through a sharing of information between the person responsible and the person harmed. Understanding and insight, empathy, and, ultimately, healing can only come about through direct or indirect communication, through restorative justice (see Figure 5.1).

Figure 5.1: The arrows chart the start of the restorative journey; empathy rises and the gap starts to close as the depth of understanding and insight increases

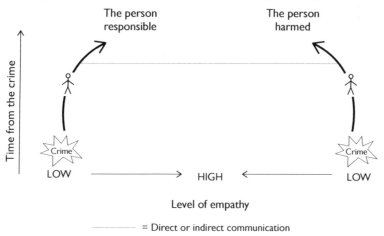

Unripe restorative justice: the danger area when it is too early for an apology or for forgiveness

In most cases, with empathy starting at rock bottom and each side thinking only of themselves, it will take time before there can be meaningful dialogue towards a restorative resolution, unless the original gap caused by the offence is very small. Time is needed for feelings to settle, and people require preparation before a restorative approach is offered. With one or both parties near the bottom of the empathy scale, this is a danger area. Care must be taken not to make things worse.

There is a misconception in some quarters that restorative justice involves marching someone round to say sorry to the person they harmed without any groundwork, expecting the other party to accept an instant apology. This is risky, and there have been one or two horror stories in which people at the bottom of the empathy scale have been involved in 'on the spot' restorative justice with disastrous consequences. In one case, police told a thief that he should go round to the house of his victim to apologise for stealing his laptop. He then made off with the replacement laptop while its owner was in the loo.[2] In another case, someone who'd been involved in a fight opted into a restorative meeting in order to have another go at the person he'd attacked.

A hollow apology

A particular danger area for restorative justice involves written 'apologies'. Information has immense power and can be used to harm; the restorative practitioner has a duty to ensure that it is handled safely. Not infrequently, a defendant is encouraged to write a 'letter of apology' by the police, their solicitors or the Crown Prosecution Service before sentence. There is a risk that the individual, who is likely still to be low on the empathy scale, may just go along with the suggestion, perhaps through false compliance or, worse, because they are told that it will look good in court.

Such a letter may be premature and will not contain an informed apology. Do they understand why they are sorry? If it is written without full acceptance of responsibility, genuine information or insight into the impact of their behaviour, and with little time or opportunity to consider the harm and its consequences, the letter may be perceived by anyone who reads it to have been written for effect. If such a letter is then sent to the person who was harmed, the sentiments may not be trusted, the words may be taken as insincere and the letter itself can be worse than meaningless – it can be experienced as an insult. On receiving their 'letter of apology', someone said: "I felt that he had been made to write the letter. It felt like a hollow apology that didn't come voluntarily and wasn't from his heart."

One young man who was robbed reflected on the three or four sentences typed and signed by the person who had robbed him. It arrived unsolicited in the post, accompanied by a covering letter from a criminal justice professional (explaining that, even if not taken well at this stage the letter could help him find closure later on in life). Perhaps unsurprisingly, he summed it all up as "a pile of shit". The apology felt to the boy like a lie – an attempt to gain forgiveness, to appease him, to excuse the offence and evade the consequences. The gesture may have been well-meaning, but because the letter arrived in the post, he had no chance to hear about the context in which it was written, to judge its genuineness or to follow it up with questions. When a clear apology is expected but is not genuinely received, when it arrives without understanding or remorse, it can feel false. The recipient may wonder: 'Are you sorry for what you have done, or sorry for getting caught?'

Cartoon 5.2: Apology letter

Premature sharing of messages is even more concerning in the Internet age, when people still smarting from a crime can retaliate by using such a letter as a weapon to humiliate the other party. In one example, the text of an apology letter that arrived unsolicited through the letterbox (which is poor practice on the part of the restorative justice practitioner) was promptly posted on Facebook to deliberately shame the perpetrator.

Just in it to be heard: can restorative justice work when people have little or no empathy?

Quite often, people near the bottom of the empathy scale wish to engage in restorative communication when their sole motivation is to express and confirm their views. In preparation interviews, they show no empathy towards the other person. There are cases where the practitioner has met with each party several times, and it becomes clear that their initial positions are unlikely to change. Can restorative justice work when people have little or no empathy?

To address the danger of making things worse, the restorative practitioner conducts a careful assessment. They try to establish people's needs and wishes, their level of empathy (and any remorse on the part of the person responsible), and their ability to take part, seeking to identify any physical or emotional risks involved. They take care to avoid over-encouraging or coercing reluctant parties into engaging in restorative justice when they may not be ready for the process or it may not be appropriate. Correctly assessing everyone's motivation is vital.

Providing the risk assessment establishes that a meeting won't make things worse, and while it won't be ideal if positions are simply confirmed or entrenched, the process may not be harmful and can still have some benefit.[3] People at Empathy Level Two – voicing – may not be ready to let go of their own narrative enough to fully hear the other side. They may not be able to soften their position to allow for gap-closing movement towards the other person, no matter what information is shared. However, a controlled and safe meeting, even if it isn't particularly restoring or reparative, may release tension and make an angry or violent confrontation at a later date less likely. This can be valuable, especially if the two people are already known to one another and likely to meet in the street anyway (possibly late at night, with one or both under the influence of alcohol). Perhaps they can agree to disagree – even to hate one another – but may be able to commit not to cause further harm. In restorative terms, a tiny bit can amount to a lot. Moreover, the success and potential benefit of a restorative process is not easy to assess and can only really be known by the participants.

Two young men had got into a knife fight over a drug debt; both ended up in court. There was no empathy between them, but they wished to meet in a controlled environment to broker a deal on safety, reassuring one another that the incident was over and there would be 'no afters'.

Cartoon 5.3: I won't hurt you...

Venting

While most people start with little or no empathy immediately after the crime, and while some remain doggedly stuck, for many, this is a temporary position. Expressing, voicing, telling the story again and again can help release the fixedness of positions. Those harmed may particularly need to be heard and be given permission to vent often violent emotions. Even a vicar may need a safe space to say 'I wish I could have him in a small room with a baseball bat' or 'If I saw her on the street, I would happily run her down'. Vengeful thoughts are sometimes expressed early on, but revenge itself is rarely a core need or motivation (although expressing those feelings may hint at other underlying needs). For those who do get hooked into revenge, there is a danger that it becomes an addictive drug that keeps their wound open and ultimately unsatisfied. In the Forgiveness Project's Annual Lecture in 2011, Clare Short said:

> "The quest for vengeance … so often inflicts harm on people who share an identity with the original perpetrator but have no guilt, and it means the evil of the original harm is recreated in the actions of the person who was wronged."

Trauma is held in the body and telling what happened again and again to someone willing to listen can help its release.[4] Where serious harm has been caused, this process may require months or years. Each time, the story may subtly shift and change. The practitioner has some powerful tools to help at this stage: deep unhurried listening; a patient acceptance of what is being expressed; empathy; being present but without an agenda; and the guided language of the restorative enquiry for those who need to talk about what happened, to feel believed. For Claire Chung, who met the man who raped her, there was release in telling her story to someone who listened without judgement. For Coral Kent, whose husband was slashed with a knife outside their home following a road rage incident, it was the relief when someone finally asked "How are you feeling?"[5]

Notes

[1] Ray and Vi's story can be found at: www.chrisdonovantrust.org/

[2] This story was quoted in *The Week*, 31 March 2012.

[3] In a restorative justice setting, a 'risk assessment' involves putting careful thought into all of the things that could go wrong when bringing people into communication – to form a list of 'what ifs' – and then considering what can be put in place to reduce the likely harm arising from each risk that has been identified. This might be done informally through conversations with colleagues, or recorded in a risk assessment document. As risk factors change over time, any risk assessment must be dynamic to meet the situation as it unfolds. A risk assessment shouldn't be used to determine which cases to exclude from a restorative process, but rather what extra support and preparation is required to make it work.

[4] The practitioner needs to be responsive to the client, and be aware when containment is required rather than encouraging them to vent, when revisiting experiences or feelings that are too painful to bear can be retraumatising. Sometimes emotions can become visceral and overwhelming, and if the client is getting out of control or dissociating (i.e. becoming detached from their immediate surroundings), the practitioner may introduce grounding techniques, such as counting backwards or focusing on objects in the room to bring attention back to the here and now. They may talk through what happened afterwards; 'It felt like it got very emotional for you…', and perhaps explore with the client whether a referral for specialist trauma counselling could be helpful.

[5] Claire's story can be found at: www.restorativejustice.org/RJOB/restorative-justice-in-a-case-of-serious-sexual-assault; Coral's story was published in the Restorative Justice Council's newsletter *Resolution* (2013) (www.restorativejustice.org).

CHAPTER SIX

Restorative enquiry

The initial approach

Figure 6.1 shows the stages in the justice system where restorative justice may be available. Regardless of where a particular case is in the system – whether the offence is minor or serious, whether it happened within the last hour or took place many years ago – the restorative journey begins with the practitioner talking with both sides separately; usually, having an appointment with the person who has committed the crime first and then ideally arranging a home visit with the person harmed. Conventional wisdom in restorative justice circles suggests that the person responsible is contacted first so that the practitioner knows whether they are willing to engage before contacting those they harmed. This avoids re-victimising the person harmed – should they be interested in a meeting only to find that the person who harmed them refuses to engage. In reality, though, the information that the other party wants a meeting is equally potent, whichever comes first.

Figure 6.1: The stages in the justice system where restorative justice may be available

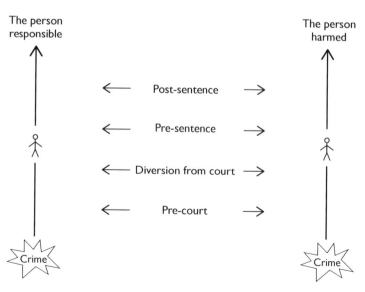

It is normally straightforward to make arrangements to meet with the person responsible, which can often be incorporated into their sentence plan or programme. Unless they are in prison, a meeting in their home can provide the practitioner with useful insights into their life, and potentially an introduction to other people who have been affected by their actions (parents, partner, siblings or other relatives).

Initial contact with people harmed by crime is more delicate and requires a careful approach. On entering the house of the person who has been harmed, the practitioner will introduce themselves, their agency and their role. They will cue into the person's demeanour and style, perhaps first asking questions or making comments that are unrelated to the offence, to ensure that they feel comfortable. Remaining receptive and alert to how the person is responding, they will then gently ask about the offence, but only if and when the person appears ready to share their experience. Coming straight out with 'the person who committed the crime against you wants to meet you' as the first thing you say (which I have witnessed happening) may not be the best technique.

Restorative enquiry

Belinda Hopkins, Director of Transforming Conflict,[1] coined the term 'restorative enquiry' to describe the form of gentle and open questioning that is used in the initial interview with both parties. Building on existing models of restorative practice, including Terry O'Connell's work in Australia, Belinda divides the restorative enquiry into five themes, and for each theme, there are questions and prompts that help the speaker to explore what happened and consider what might help them to move forward.

Theme 1: Telling the story

In this part of the conversation, the speaker is simply invited to share their story of their experience, in their own words and in whatever way they feel most comfortable telling it. The practitioner starts off by saying: 'Would you like to tell me what happened?' In Theme 1, the practitioner uses active listening skills to help the speaker to talk freely and feel heard, occasionally encouraging them to continue with their narrative through prompts, such as: 'What happened next?'; 'Hmmm'; 'And then ...?'

Theme 2: Exploring thoughts and feelings

Often, the speaker's story spills out in great detail, and the practitioner may only chip in occasionally if at all. Deep insights may be shared, and the listener may get a clear picture simply from that initial question. Regardless of how the story is told, it can then be helpful to look back again over the whole experience, with the practitioner inviting the speaker to consider what was going on for them at particular points in their narrative. The practitioner will identify several key moments and ask the speaker what they were thinking and then what they were feeling at that time. Taking an imaginary case of someone who was robbed, the practitioner's questioning might go along these lines:

Rob (the practitioner): "Can you remember what you were thinking when you were sitting on the bus before the robbery happened?"

Bethan (the person harmed): "Before it happened? I was thinking ... I was thinking 'I can't wait to get home – this has been the longest day ever.'"

Rob: "And how were you feeling?"

Bethan: "Pretty tired. College always took it out of me."

Rob: "And then, at the moment when you first became aware that the young men were sitting behind you, do you remember what were you thinking?"

Bethan: "I was thinking, like, 'Why did you choose the seat right behind me?'"

Rob: "And how did you feel?"

Bethan: "A bit freaked out if I'm honest."

Rob: "And then when one of the young men said he had a knife and told you to hand over your cash and your phone, what were you thinking at that moment?"

Bethan: "I was thinking 'Oh my God! He's going to stab me!' You know, I really thought I was going to die that day."

Rob: "You were thinking 'He's going to stab you...' And what were you feeling inside?"

Bethan: "I was just terrified!"

Rob: [Leaves a silence.] "And then, straight after the bus had stopped and the young men had run off, can you remember what was going through your head at that moment?"

Bethan: "'Oh shit! I've just been robbed!' Then I thought 'They took my phone and I can't even phone my mum...'"

Rob: "And feeling?"

Bethan: "I remember literally shaking with shock. I felt sick. You know, thinking back, I also felt really embarrassed, like it was all my fault or something?"

Rob: "Embarrassed?"[2]

Bethan: "Yeah. I know it sounds strange but I feel a bit ashamed, as if it was me who did something wrong. Thinking about it, I don't know why I should be the one feeling ashamed..."

Rob: "Hmmm... [leaves a silence] Looking back over the whole experience, what are your thoughts on it all now?"

Bethan: "I still think about it every time I go out. I keep looking over my shoulder. I'm like wondering if I might see them coming round a corner or something."

Rob: "And feeling?"

Bethan: "To be honest, I'm still really, really angry about it."

Taking the speaker back over their narrative and exploring their thoughts and feelings can help them to process their experience, and express and perhaps vent some difficult thoughts and emotions. If it is the person responsible speaking, they may also make connections between their thinking, their feelings and their choices on the day of their offence. For both, it can be a great relief to be heard by a professional who is alert and present, attentive and curious, simply wishing to hear about their thoughts and feelings surrounding the crime and its aftermath.

Theme 3: Considering the impact

The practitioner now asks the speaker to consider who has been affected by the crime, and how. People in restorative justice circles often speak of the 'ripples of harm' that a crime causes, and, here, the speaker can identify just how far those ripples have reached. In addition to the people directly involved, the impact of the crime can spread to witnesses and bystanders, friends and family members, professionals, and neighbourhoods and communities.

Theme 4: Exploring needs

Having allowed the speaker to share what happened and consider who has been affected, the next question is: 'What do you need now to feel better?' Needs are of critical importance in restorative justice. So often, we express our needs as ideal solutions that we project onto the other: if only someone else would do something different, our lives would be perfect. 'What I need is for him to …', 'You should …', 'I think you need to …' – these are positional statements. If the answer to 'What do you need to feel better?' is expressed as 'I need him/her to …', it could be perceived as a demand, and if expressed in a restorative meeting, it would elicit a defensive reaction. The practitioner, hearing 'needs to' rather than 'needs for', may gently rephrase the point made by saying 'It sounds like what you need is …', helping the speaker to identify the need underlying that position. The practitioner will help the speaker to explore, identify and name their needs, using supplementary questions to try to get below the positions and demands that may be expressed, to the underlying needs. It could sound something like this:

Rob: "What do you need to feel better, Bethan?"

Bethan: "To feel better? Me? I'd feel better if someone told me that the guy who robbed me has been mugged at knifepoint by the other prisoners."

Rob: "Mugged at knifepoint?"

Bethan: "Right!"

Rob: "What is it about him being mugged by the other prisoners that would help you feel better?"

Bethan: "Well, then he would know what I've been through."

Rob: "Okay … you're thinking that he doesn't know what it's been like for you."

Bethan: "How could he? No one does. It's been a living hell."

Rob: "So, no one knows what you've been through. It sounds perhaps like you need some recognition?"

Bethan: "Recognition? You mean like people knowing how I feel? I don't know. No one thinks about the victims. No one knows what we have to go through. I got nothing. No help, nothing."

Rob: "So, it sounds like you also need support?"

Bethan: "That would be nice. You know, I've had to cope with this all on my own? Meanwhile, he'll get all the support he needs when he gets out. No one appreciates how hard it is to get your life back together."

Rob: [Leaves a silence.] "Okay. So you need recognition of what you've been through, and also support. You also just mentioned appreciation, too. What else might help you to feel better?"

Bethan: "This is going to sound awful, but I'd feel a lot better if he'd just drop down dead. … I can't believe I just said that!"

Rob: "So, can I ask – what is it about him dropping down dead that would help you to feel better?"

Bethan: "Well, I don't really want him to be dead, but if he was, I guess I would know for sure that he will never attack me again."

Rob: "Oh … So it sounds like you need to feel safe."

Bethan: "Yes, that's right. Because I know that he'll come out at some point, and I keep thinking that he might still be after me – you know, he could be blaming me for the police being called, for him getting in so much trouble."

Rob: "So, you're thinking that maybe he might be planning to attack you when he is released, but you're not sure. It sounds like you need some reassurance?"

Bethan: "Reassurance?… Maybe … yes. I need to know that he isn't going to hurt me again. Sometimes, I'm awake all night worrying about when he comes out. What if I bump into him in the street?"

Rob: "Okay, so we have identified some of your needs – for recognition, support, appreciation, safety and also reassurance, thinking about when he comes out. Have I got that right? Is there anything else that might help you feel better?"

Bethan: "Well yeah, I think that he should know that it's right out of order to go round robbing people. I felt a complete fool handing over all my stuff. Like a lot of young kids these days – they just don't care, they take what they want, just treat other people like dirt. No consideration, no manners."

Rob: "So, I think you are saying that you also need respect …"

Marshall Rosenberg has identified the needs expressed here – for recognition, support, appreciation, safety, reassurance and respect – as 'basic human needs that we all share'.[3] If the practitioner uses the hints that the speaker drops in their narrative to accurately point to a basic human need, it can feel to them like a light bulb moment. Respect? That is *exactly* what I need! If the practitioner gets it wrong, no matter: the speaker will either ignore them or put them right.

Theme 5: Ways forward

What can help to move things forward? The benefit of clearly identifying the speaker's needs is that they lead neatly into Theme 5, which is next steps: 'So, you said you need support – how might that need be met?'; 'There was a need for safety and reassurance, what might that look like?' Helping both parties name the needs that have arisen out of the offence is crucial to successful restorative practice. If they spontaneously come up with the idea of a restorative process to meet their needs, which often happens, the practitioner can simply enthuse: 'What an interesting idea! I am sure we can explore that …' If the idea can come straight from them, it is much more powerful than the practitioner spelling out restorative justice as a menu of options. They will talk themselves into restorative justice – without the practitioner ever needing to mention it.

If the parties do meet, there is another benefit of getting to the level of basic human needs, beyond assessing where the speaker is at on their journey. The format of the restorative meeting itself is identical to the restorative enquiry described here, with both parties exploring each of the five themes in turn. It won't be fruitful if at the point in the meeting where the facilitator says 'What do you need to feel better?', the answer comes back: 'I would feel better if you burned in hell' or 'I need you to drop down dead'. Those sentiments are natural parts of the venting process and belong in that initial enquiry. If the practitioner helps focus this part of the conversation on the basic human needs that underlie those positions, statements and demands – needs that are universal – everyone in the room will be able to recognise and see that they also have those same needs. There can then be genuine sharing and cooperation, as everyone joins together in exploring and addressing their needs, finding a way forward that helps everyone to feel better.

During these initial contacts, the practitioner will model qualities that help insight and empathy. They will show respect, remain non-judgemental, be scrupulously honest and take great care with confidentiality and the ownership of information. People respond when approached by someone who embodies these values, where they feel treated with empathy and respect, because they need empathy for themselves before they can feel it for others.

The made-up conversations in the previous section may feel a little unreal and the procession of questions from the practitioner somewhat rigid. In a real-life situation, the questions and answers arise naturally, and the speaker is led fluidly through the five themes – sharing their experience, exploring their needs and expressing their wishes for the future – without realising that there is a clear logic behind the process.

It really does work, and it is common for the person responsible or person harmed to express a desire to engage in restorative justice by the end of the interview. If there is a good match, with both parties interested, it can really feel like both parties are walking towards one another with open arms, eager to close the gap.

Cartoon 6.1: It can really feel like both parties are walking towards one another with open arms...

Most cases do not unfold quite as smoothly as this, however, and the practitioner may have some more work to do to identify particular keys that might encourage people to enter a restorative process, and some barriers or blocks to participation that may have to be removed before people will agree to a meeting.

Notes

[1] Transforming Conflict is the leading organisation in the UK for restorative approaches in schools and other youth settings.

[2] The technique of repeating back a key word as a question can sometimes be helpful. It shows that the practitioner is listening carefully and with curiosity, and can sometimes elicit a deeper reflection and insight from the speaker.

[3] Rosenberg, M. (1999) *Nonviolent communication*, Encinitas, CA: Puddledancer Press.

CHAPTER SEVEN

The keys and blocks to restorative justice

Taking responsibility

The first block that can thwart the natural impulse we all have to close the gaps we create with others is the common tendency to deny or justify our harmful actions, to become defensive, to avoid taking responsibility. The concept of 'responsibility' is a crucial and complex theme for restorative justice, and in this book, I will identify three aspects to the term.[1] This first one looks back to what happened and says: 'Yes, I admit that I did my part in it, I was responsible' (the other two come later). A restorative approach isn't possible if the perpetrator flatly denies involvement. 'I wasn't there' is not going to work as a starting position in a restorative meeting. If they *were* there, it may be possible to build from this position, to help them identify which parts of the incident they were responsible for – even if it is only their failure to stop it happening. Taking responsibility for wrongdoing is difficult and painful, as we try to ward off feeling bad by shielding our inner 'soft spot' with defensive thinking. In Chapter Two, we considered how people who offend often minimise the impact of their actions ('They were insured anyway – it won't cost them anything'), shift the blame ('She had been winding me up all day'), deny their involvement ('He just fell over – I didn't push him'), deny that they had self-control ('I just saw red') or insist that they were entitled ('Everybody else has one, why shouldn't I?').

It can be hard to challenge a tendency to 'blame the victim', either for bringing the crime upon themselves (for leaving a window open, looking at someone the wrong way, spreading rumours on the web, going out with the wrong girl or boy, starting the fight) or for 'grassing' and getting others in trouble. Many people who offend are masters at playing down and minimising their actions and set about dehumanising the person they hurt. Even if the person responsible appears to have this strongly entrenched attitude, a restorative meeting may not be impossible, although the person harmed will be warned not to expect too much – and may not want to go ahead.

Taking responsibility is particularly challenging for younger people if their criminal activities are encouraged or condoned by their parents. In his autobiography *The damage done*, Peter Woolf explains how he came to become a 'career criminal', stuck in a perpetual cycle of drugs, violent crime and prison (the remarkable story of the restorative meeting that transformed his life is told in later chapters). Peter describes how as a child, his family would praise him for committing burglaries and that his grandfather's motto was: 'If they can't hang onto it, they don't deserve it.'[2] Some children are taught by their parents or peers to objectify and dehumanise other people (often specific categories, such as women or people from other backgrounds and cultures). These are the cases where the criminal justice experts will be thinking: 'Well, what chance did s/he have?'

It's not a lost cause in every case. One young man talked about how when he was a boy, his father would take him along as a lookout when he committed burglaries. Later on, when he had started doing burglaries of his own, the young man was horrified to learn that one of the houses he turned over belonged to an elderly gentleman. He decided that he wanted to meet the owner, reflecting that this man might be like his own grandfather, who was frail and living alone. The young man faced intense opposition to the idea from his family – and most of all from his own father, who simply couldn't (or wouldn't) understand why he would want to meet someone he'd burgled.

Most crimes are committed in the company of others, and it is often true that the person caught is not fully or solely responsible for what happened. Sometimes, that person has been scapegoated, or has chosen to take the rap rather than inform on others who were involved. Unfortunately, many hide behind those reasons and turn them into excuses, which can be a major block to a successful restorative process. Restorative practitioners can help the perpetrator to map out their area of responsibility, to identify where they lie on a continuum from totally to marginally culpable. They will shift the emphasis away from what they *don't* feel responsible for (the actions of others, provocation from the person who was harmed, the need for food because they were homeless, the influence of alcohol or drugs) by identifying the part they fully accept and probably regret (their own part in what happened, responding to provocation with greater violence, taking what wasn't theirs, drinking so much they can't remember what happened). For Stephen, one of the young men who murdered Ray and Vi Donovan's son, Christopher, taking responsibility came as a relief:

> In order to move on in my life I had to face up to the death of Christopher, take responsibility for the person I was then and try to develop myself to lead a more positive life. I found that the more I took responsibility the better I felt inside.[3]

From responsibility to empathy

For the perpetrator, taking responsibility in the sense of acknowledging what they have done is a crucial first step in readiness for restorative justice. However, some may fully admit to their crime yet feel no regret or remorse for the harm they have caused.

This may be thoughtlessness rather than deliberate cruelty. It might not have occurred to them to think about consequences. The practitioner may be able to raise their empathy quickly through clever questioning:

> 'Do you know the person you harmed?'
> 'Have you seen him/her since?'
> 'What did his/her face look like?'
> 'What did the house/car/store look like?'
> 'Who do you think lived in the house?'
> 'How were they affected?'
> 'What do you think they felt?'
> 'Who else was affected?'
> 'What do you think happened to them? How have they been harmed?'
> 'How do you think they feel?'
> 'How do you think you would feel?'

A 'one-step removed' technique using 'What if …?' questions can help the upwards shift in empathy: 'What if it was your house that was burgled?'; 'How would you feel if your younger brother was assaulted?'

For others, the lack of empathy has deeper roots. We have seen how empathy, or rather its absence, plays a crucial role in offending. Many people who commit crimes will have received little empathy themselves, and show little or no empathy as they hurt others.

Kay Pranis describes the conditions for empathy to develop as follows:

- Regular feedback about how our actions are affecting others, respectfully communicated.
- Relationships in which we are valued and our worth is validated.
- Experience of sympathy from others when we are in pain.[4]

Given these favourable conditions, empathy develops naturally in childhood or early adolescence as we learn to see beyond our own self-centred bubble of existence and begin to understand and share the feelings of others. Many people who offend won't have received these early socialisation experiences within their family and community. They weren't given a sense of their own worth, no one taught them to understand how all things are interconnected and they didn't learn to consider the impact of their actions on others.

Even so, restorative practitioners have great faith that empathy can be learnt, at any age, and have created specific programmes for this purpose. They believe that developing a capacity for empathy can contribute directly to preventing future victimisation. It may also encourage the person responsible to enter into a restorative process.

'What have I done?' The value of victim empathy courses

There are many victim empathy courses around, including the Forgiveness Project's RESTORE programme, Restorative Thinking courses and groups organised locally by youth offending teams, probation services and prisons. One of the most successful is the eight-week Sycamore Tree programme organised by the Prison Fellowship, which is delivered in many prisons throughout the world.[5]

Before confronting them with the consequences of their own behaviour, victim empathy courses often start by exploring the perpetrators' own experiences of victimisation. In this delicate work, the practitioner helps the participant to use insight into their own suffering to start to develop self-empathy. If people have the courage to recognise and share the impact that crime has had on themselves, particularly in a group context, they may receive empathy from others who have been through similar experiences. The practitioner will also model empathy and compassion, so that the person responsible can begin to sense what they might have needed when they were the one harmed, as a first step to avoiding inflicting future pain on others. One young person found this a turning point:

> We were ... told to think back to a time in our lives when we had been a victim. This made me think back to when I was 15 years old and experiencing a lot of violence, which was a really difficult time for me. It was at this point that I can honestly say I was truly sorry for my actions and felt bad for what I had done to my victim. In my mind I was thinking 'how could I do something so bad to someone

else without even thinking about their feelings?' It also made me realize how things, like an assault, can change a person's life forever.[6]

The next step is to provide feedback about how their crime has affected others. If information isn't available to provide real insight into the actual damage they caused, the person responsible should be challenged – with the help of the group – to consider their actions carefully and imagine what the impact *might* have been. In Oxfordshire Youth Offending Service, a programme called the Assault Awareness Course arranges for young people whose crimes involved violence to meet medical staff at the Accident and Emergency (A&E) Department of the local hospital to bring to life the real or potential consequences of their actions for the person they injured. During the session, they create a full-size outline picture of a person (drawing round one another on lining paper) and add the cuts, bruises, broken bones or other wounds they inflicted. They then take their pictures to A&E to learn from the medics how this may have affected their victim. In the next session, the young people are taken to the Headway charity and introduced to someone who suffered serious head injury following a violent assault. These initiatives can drive home the point that the difference between a blow that leaves a bruise and one that causes permanent injury or death can be very small.

Some of the young people attending this programme are deeply affected. At the end of her course, the young person quoted earlier wrote:

> Since being part of the Assault Awareness Course it has made me open my eyes to other people's feelings. There is a lot more to life than I thought. Sometimes I don't know how lucky I am and take things for granted. I don't want to be known as a criminal. I am disappointed in myself, but proud that I have completed the course and learnt things that I did not know before. I feel that I went home a completely different person, and not just for that day, but forever. Most importantly the Assault Awareness Course has made me feel like I can finally leave my offending behind and start my new life.[7]

Evaluations show an 80% increase in victim empathy, and the programme has a positive impact on reoffending rates.[8] It seldom leads to gloating, and frequently to reflection and remorse.

Some victim empathy courses use theoretical information and case studies or newspaper clippings to try to challenge the perpetrator by exploring the damage caused by other people's crimes. This can be helpful, although learning second-hand about the impact of other people's crimes can sometimes lack impact and may miss that helpful movement that comes through insight into the genuine (if, at this stage, hypothetical) consequences of one's own actions. Someone with low empathy who is adept at shifting the blame will claim that their offense was *completely* different to the one described in the case study or news story – even if to anyone else, the difference is insignificant. If they robbed a man and are given a case example to work on where someone robbed a woman, it won't have much of an impact: 'I would *never* rob a woman, you'd have to be sick to do that.'

Cartoon 7.1: ...nothing like my crime...

Many areas use 'surrogate victims' – inviting people who have been harmed by crime to meet participants on victim empathy courses to provide them with an insight into the harm that crime can cause. Hearing a first-hand account of the impact of an offence, even though it wasn't related to their own crime, can have an impact, and is, in some cases, pivotal to the person responsible changing their own attitude and behaviour. Marian Partington's sister Lucy was abducted and murdered by Fred and Rosemary West.[9] A local man who had committed burglaries heard Marian talk during a victim empathy course at Bristol prison. Afterwards, he told his warders, "Please call the police. I want to return all the things I have stolen to their owners – there are burglaries I haven't been caught for," even though he knew he would get extra time in prison.

Putting themselves forward to share their story in such programmes can be equally helpful for the people harmed. Terry Brown, Head of Programme Development at the Prison Fellowship,[10] tells of a shop-owner who attended a Sycamore Tree course to share her experience of having her premises burgled. "The hardest part of the experience for me", she told the group of 20 prisoners, "was that the charity box was taken from the counter." One of the prisoners looked increasingly uncomfortable and suddenly said:

> "I'm so sorry, I have stolen charity boxes. Not that I was the person who burgled you personally, but I have burgled other shops. I thought the charity box was just a plastic tube full of money waiting for me. I'm so sorry for what I did."

The shop-owner then realised that she had been waiting to hear the word 'sorry'. At last, she had found relief from a burden she had been carrying for many years. Ray and Vi Donovan also found their involvement in victim empathy courses helpful: 'This was the first time since their 18 year old son Christopher was murdered in 2001 that they felt they had a voice and that the prisoners were thinking, feeling human beings, just like them.'[11]

Careful use of victim empathy work can encourage reflection for those responsible, can help to generate greater insight and empathy, and form part of the preparation for a restorative process (see Figure 7.1).

There is a convincing argument for victim empathy work to be mandatory for those people who commit crime and show little understanding of the consequences of their offences or remorse for the damage they cause. If we think of empathy as a ladder, it is almost as if some people need a leg up to reach the bottom rung, to the point where some reflection and insight creep in. A victim empathy course can help them 'see', to acknowledge (rather than conveniently forget) the person they harmed. Without it, many simply won't consider or recognise how other people are affected by their actions. In the Donovan's case, a victim empathy course provided the key to the restorative process:

Figure 7.1: Victim empathy work as part of preparation for restorative justice, with the person responsible developing their insight and empathy

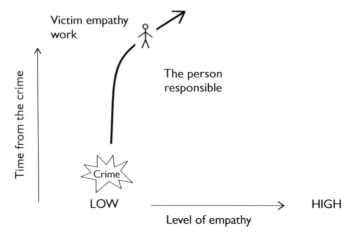

One of the [group of youths who beat Ray and Vi Donovan's son, Christopher, to death] admitted to the Donovans that for the first two years of his eight year sentence he didn't spare a thought for the victims of his crimes. But after he took part in a victim empathy course in prison, he says he couldn't get Chris out of his 'head and heart' and he felt an urgent need to apologise to the Donovans.[12]

Having developed some empathy, ideally, the power of restorative justice will simply take over, and the person responsible will want to carry on climbing up the ladder, leading them to the point where they come up with the restorative idea themselves.

Terry Brown tells of meeting a prisoner at the start of one of the Sycamore Tree programmes he was tutoring. Although Terry hadn't asked for information about the participants' offences, this prisoner wanted him to know that he was a drug baron, and that he had 'customers' and not 'victims': "I sell drugs to the rich and famous. It is their choice to buy my drugs. They are customers, not victims." When asked if the customers ever sold on the drugs, he shrugged: "Sometimes." Terry asked: "What if the last person down the line is a teenage girl?" "So?" "What if she is lying face down in the gutter?" "Not my problem." "What if you turn her over and discover it is your own daughter?" The prisoner bristled, and Terry automatically took two steps backwards, thinking: "I've gone too far this time." At the end of the course, the man approached Terry again and said: "Do you realise how close you came to having your head knocked off when you said that thing about my daughter?" Terry replied: "Yes – that's why I stepped back." "Well I want you to know that what you said was the biggest wake-up call of my life, it changed everything. I do have victims."

What about people with zero empathy?

In Chapter One, we touched on Baron-Cohen's assertion that, in severe cases, childhood trauma may lead to people reaching adulthood with 'zero degrees of empathy'. He argues that zero empathy can develop into a stable personality trait that becomes fixed and enduring. Anyone working in criminal justice will have met the occasional client who is cognitively aware of the harm they cause others, but are not affectively connected to their experience. There are individuals who may simply be unsuited to victim empathy training or restorative justice, because there is too great a risk of them 'getting off' on other people's suffering.

While a limited capacity for empathy can help to explain how a crime came about, it is not an excuse. With the exception of those (very) few who may never be suitable, low empathy may not rule out either victim empathy work or a restorative process. It takes a lot for a restorative practitioner to give up. Baron-Cohen opens up the possibility even for zero empathy to be 'treated', suggesting 'forms of role-play that involve taking the victims' perspective'[13] (which is an exercise often found in victim empathy courses). It is all the more important to try victim empathy interventions with people who have zero empathy, as they are the most likely to reoffend. Moreover, empathy works in mysterious ways, as shown in the example described in the Introduction, where the desire to engage in restorative justice spread contagiously among a group of prisoners.

Baron-Cohen also talks about people who appear to be wired up differently from birth, who may present as unempathetic even in adulthood. People on the autistic spectrum can seem cold and uncaring, and may appear to have little or no empathy. Baron-Cohen's research indicates that people with autistic spectrum conditions have an underactive empathy circuit, partly because for many autistic people, other people's behaviour is simply beyond comprehension: they are unable to identify others' feelings. However the term 'autistic spectrum' encompasses a wide range of conditions and symptoms, and for some, the affective element of empathy may be intact, but they are unable to communicate their empathetic response in a way that will be recognised by others – particularly in a stressful situation.

The restorative justice practitioner must be careful not to assume that where an empathetic response isn't apparent, the person they are with has no empathy. Practitioners need to have a creative and inclusive mindset to enable everyone to have equal access to their service, and in these cases, they can be imaginative, perhaps breaking the process into small sections, coaching the person in how they wish to share their narrative, using different media such as cartoons, art materials, puppets and video to help them engage (bearing in mind that lots of autistic people are visual thinkers). It may also be important to brief the person harmed; they may need to give more, and be ready to receive less. If the person who offended against them is autistic, they may need to know that autism affects the way that a person communicates and relates to people around them, and that an empathy response that may be hidden, or appears forced and insincere – for example, an apology delivered in a flat tone without emotion or tears – can in fact be heartfelt and genuine.

Keys for the person responsible

Once the perpetrator is taking responsibility and starting to show empathy, two of the major blocks to restorative justice have been removed. They are beginning to see the individual they harmed as a real person. As they start to consider what they might do to repair the harm they caused, it may slowly dawn on them that restorative justice is far tougher than anything else in the criminal justice system:

> These can be deeply difficult encounters, requiring more soul searching and acceptance than they may ever have shown before. Many, not surprisingly, find it very hard; they would much rather be in the familiar comfort of a court. Is it soft? Hardly.[14]

In court, an advocate speaks for them, trying to mitigate their responsibility. Once sentenced, they may find it preferable simply to bear their punishment. It's easier to see the matter through without engaging with the reality of what they have done, or giving it only cursory consideration – certainly, it's easier without facing those they affected. Sadly, many people who commit crime get away without being held to account for their wrongdoing by the people who matter most – the individuals they harmed. Punishment is not genuine accountability.

Repairing the harm caused through offending is a stated objective of the justice system,[15] and should be a central feature (*the* central feature?) of all plans and sentences for people who cause harm. Encouraging a perpetrator to engage in a restorative process is much easier if it is presented as a normal and expected part of their programme, so that the question is not 'Are you willing to repair the harm you caused?', but '*How* are you going to repair the harm you caused?'; not 'Would you like to?', but '*How* do you see that happening?' It is helpful to normalise the process, and everyone who speaks to the person responsible – police, solicitors, magistrates, judges and case workers – can reinforce the message. Most people who have caused harm, get it – it isn't complicated to explain. If you're the one who spilt the milk, it is your mess, your responsibility. How are you going to clear it up? Do you need help?

Notes

[1.] The three aspects of responsibility were introduced in Wallis, P., Aldington, C. and Liebmann, M. (2010) *What have I done? A victim empathy programme for young people*, London: Jessica Kingsley Publishers.

[2.] Woolf, P. (2008) *The damage done*, London: Bantam Books.

[3.] Extract from a letter written by Stephen, one of the young men who murdered Christopher Donovan, 'Restorative justice – what it meant to me' (www.chrisdonovantrust.org/restorative-justice.php).

[4.] Pranis, K. (2000) 'Empathy development in youth through restorative practices', *Public Service Psychology*, vol 25, no 2, p 1.

[5.] A three-year research programme by Cambridge University is currently under way to measure the efficacy of the Sycamore Tree in helping to reduce reoffending behaviour.

[6.] Wallis, P., McLellan, L., Clothier, K. and Malpass, J. (2013) 'The Assault Awareness Course and New Drivers' Initiative; groupwork programmes for young people convicted of violent and vehicle offences', *Groupwork*, vol 23, no 3, pp 63-71.

[7.] See note 6.

[8.] See note 6. Empathy is measured using a psychometric questionnaire that participants complete at the start and end of the course.

[9.] See Marian Partington's book listed in Further Reading, p 197.

[10.] These stories were shared during a talk by Terry on the Sycamore Tree project as part of a series of lectures on restorative justice held at Worcester College, Oxford, on 8 March 2012. They are reproduced with permission.

[11.] www.chrisdonovantrust.org/restorative-justice.php

[12.] http://tinyurl.com/og56npf

[13.] Baron-Cohen, S. (2012) *Zero degrees of empathy*, London: Penguin, p 105.

[14.] From an Opinion article by Macdonald, K. (2010) 'Stop dumping children in warehouse prisons', *The Times*, 15 July, p 21.

[15.] The Ministry of Justice website explains the objectives of the criminal justice system as follows: 'The legal system must uphold fairness in society: both in business and for individuals. We want to ensure justice for victims of crime and better rehabilitation for criminals, with a reduction in the rate of reoffending. The justice system must punish the guilty, protect our liberties and rehabilitate offenders. *We will ensure that more criminals make amends to victims and communities for the harm they have caused and help them break the destructive cycle of crime*' (emphasis added). www.gov.uk/government/topics/law-and-the-justice-system

CHAPTER EIGHT

Choice, encouragement or coercion?

There is a lot of debate in the restorative justice literature about choice and coercion in the restorative process. Some would argue that restorative justice has to be fully voluntary all round, and that to exert pressure for either side to engage is inappropriate and potentially harmful.

What is clear and accepted by everyone is that the person harmed should never be made to feel obliged to take part. The worst sin in restorative circles is to push for the involvement of the people harmed for the benefit of those responsible (although one of the most common motivations for people harmed to choose restorative justice is from a desire to help 'their' perpetrator to learn from the experience). Getting the right balance of information and encouragement so that those harmed can make an informed choice is vital to successful restorative justice. It should always be made clear that this is a neutral offer – with lots of reminders that there is no pressure for them to take it up.

It is always going to be best if those who commit crime also opt in voluntarily. It's more powerful for the person harmed to be told that the person who caused them harm is hoping to meet them, and that it is that person's genuine and free choice to engage in restorative justice. Those harmed will always want to know if the meeting is voluntary or compulsory, and whether by opting in, the perpetrator's punishment will be reduced. As Walgrave notes: 'the quality of restoration will decisively improve if the offender co-operates freely'.[1]

The problem arises with those people who have caused harm but don't wish to make amends, even with encouragement. If restorative justice practitioners insist that involvement is completely voluntary, the scope of restorative justice will be limited. Asked if they would like to repay, many will say 'No thanks', and be on their way. It would be possible to keep the value base of 'voluntariness' pure, deliver restorative justice for those who choose it and simply leave the rest to punishment from the criminal justice system. This would, Walgrave asserts, consign restorative justice to 'a marginal addendum to the criminal justice system'.[2]

The alternative is for there to be some form of pressure on those who have caused harm and don't feel inclined to put it right. Some authors (see Braithwaite[3] and Crawford and Newburn[4]) argue that effective restorative justice may depend upon coercion. Others point out the fact that being arrested and/or convicted of an offence and then asked to participate in restorative justice is in itself a form of coercion. Once in the court process, restorative justice sits within a system where freedom is restricted. In youth justice, the person responsible must plead guilty to receive a Referral Order, but once sentenced, their failure to comply in the restorative process could lead to a more punitive sanction. The Crime & Courts Act 2013 allows for courts to defer sentence for a restorative process – which could (if successful) have an impact on a defendant's sentence, even potentially keeping them out of prison. If reparation agreements are signed, there can be repercussions for non-compliance. There is already a lot of coercion for people in the criminal justice system to take part and repay society; offender participation is rarely wholly voluntary.

Howard Zehr takes a more moral stance, suggesting that it is appropriate to 'oblige' the person responsible to engage: 'crime is a violation of people and interpersonal relationships, violations create obligations, [and] the central obligation is to put right the wrongs'.[5] The question now becomes: how much pressure is appropriate, and what happens to the most reluctant?

A continuum of voluntariness

Box 8.1 introduces 'a continuum of voluntariness'. It is important to start with an open mind and always try at first to see whether the person responsible will opt in voluntarily. The restorative enquiry described earlier avoids judgement and helps that person to share their story, to explore all their thoughts and feelings around their crime, and to consider the consequences for those they have harmed. Done skilfully, this can help the speaker to see that many of their offence-related needs could be met through a restorative process.

For those remaining reluctant, the practitioner, while edging up the continuum towards coercion, can still allow some measure of choice, even within a system that takes choice away: 'You are expected to do something to make amends for the harm you caused. What that looks like is down to you.' There is a bottom line. Most would agree that it is appropriate to insist that the person responsible at least hear about the harm they caused (if those they harmed wish to share this information), and be expected to consider how they might make amends.

Attempts to go further and compel people to engage in direct restorative justice have to be treated with extreme care. They can backfire. Putting a reluctant perpetrator in the same room as the people

---

Box 8.1: The options: 'a continuum of voluntariness'

1. *Compulsion* – 'You have to do this even if you are really against it'
2. *Coercion* – 'You should do this'
3. *Opt out* – 'This is going to happen unless you opt out'
4. *Encouragement* – 'It could be really good if you do this'
5. *Neutral offer* – 'This is available if you are interested'
6. *Opt in* – 'If you are interested you will have to let us know'
7. *Poor offer* – 'You probably won't want to do this'
8. *Not offered* – 'We don't do restorative justice here'

This list shows the range of ways in which a restorative justice service might be offered to the person responsible, the person harmed or both.

---

they have harmed risks making matters worse. If tried, it will require lots of preparation and demand the highest level of skill and care from the practitioner. It can work. Providing the person harmed knows clearly what to expect, they might gain something – even if it's just seeing 'who done it'.

A healthy journey through the continuum of voluntariness for the person responsible could look something like that in Box 8.2.

Box 8.2: A healthy continuum of voluntariness

Step 1. Compulsion

- 'You have to meet the Restorative Justice Worker to talk about your offence and find out about restorative justice.'
- 'You have to engage in a victim empathy course to consider the harm that your actions have caused to others.'

Step 2. Coercion

- 'You should be willing to hear how you affected the person you hurt, either through meeting with the Restorative Justice Worker who has met that person, or via a Victim Impact Statement.'

Step 3. Encouragement

- 'It could be really good if you answer any questions or concerns the person you hurt may have: face to face in a restorative meeting, through indirect messages or in writing.'
- 'You are encouraged to communicate with the person you harmed, and there are many potential benefits for both of you.'

Step 4. Neutral offer

- 'You will be given choice in how this happens.'

This shows how a restorative justice intervention could be introduced to the person responsible, to allow some choice in a system where their freedom is constrained.

Sometimes, even a meeting where the person responsible is forced to attend can have positive outcomes. One young man on a Referral Order was told that the man whose jaw he broke in a fight would be attending his panel meeting – whether he liked it or not (he didn't). During the panel, he kept to his line that the man deserved it for being aggressive and "in his face". The 'victim' said that he was sorry for his part in the incident, explaining that his partner had died only two days before, and that he had been drinking to try to "get out of his head." He then said he felt he also deserved an apology, and to his credit, the 'offender' apologised. To the amazement of his parents and the panel, both stood up and solemnly shook hands.

Even when people freely choose restorative justice, the motivation may not be quite what it appears. Peter Woolf, who was mentioned on page 90 (he received praise from his family for his offending) met Will Riley, whose house he had burgled. He said afterwards that he agreed to the meeting partly to get out of his prison cell (and the promise from one of the staff that there would be a packet of Hobnob biscuits).[6] A colleague shared the story of a man who inadvertently caused another man's death by crushing him behind gates during a getaway. He met the man's widow, and only later admitted that he did so in the hope of improving his parole prospects. In fact, the meeting freed him from a nightmare of guilt and shame that had stopped him from sleeping and eating. The outcomes from both these meetings have been profound and life-changing for all involved.

Finally, the power imbalance inherent in any professional–client relationship can lead people to do or say things that they think they 'should' do or say. This can lead the person harmed to engage from a sense of guilt or obligation. It can lead the person responsible to engage through false compliance, which may lead to unpleasant surprises later on; if they are insincere, if their apology is forced, if it is obvious that they are not really interested in being involved or resent being there, it can make things worse for the person they harmed. Young people may be more vulnerable than adults to persuasion against their will and the line between encouraging and compelling a young person to enter into the process of restorative justice is a fine one.

Some restorative services monitor and compare 'conversion rates': the percentage of each practitioner's caseload that result in a face-to-face meeting. Recognising that you have to count something and that a service with no face-to-face meetings must be doing something wrong, targets and Key Performance Indicators (KPIs) for restorative justice carry the risk that practitioners may feel that they should be achieving meetings in more of their cases, increasing the pressure on them and on their clients. If they end up getting someone in the room that they have to really convince, the restorative meeting isn't likely to be successful.

What's in it for me?

In order to encourage the person responsible to engage, it may help to map out what's in it for them – to ask what will help them feel better. Box 8.3 shows some of the benefits of restorative justice for the person who has caused harm.

Box 8.3: Potential benefits of restorative justice for the person who has caused harm

- *To get it out, tell their story, confess to the person they hurt.* Voicing the story is as important if you have caused hurt as it is if you have been hurt. In one restorative meeting, a man who had taken another's life ruminated upon the incident every day in prison. Finally, he had the opportunity to meet his victim's partner in a restorative meeting. Both had a great need to talk about what had happened. When it came to his turn, holding her hands, he told his story in minute detail and with great intensity, starting each sentence: "I remember.... I remember...." This was cathartic for him, and important for her, as it filled gaps in her knowledge of what happened in the last moments of her partner's life.
- *To show themselves in a better light.* Most people who commit a crime regret the harm they have caused (when they stop to think about it), and many value an opportunity to separate the deed from themselves as a person: 'That isn't me really'; 'I'm not like that'; 'I'm not just some yob'; 'Obviously, I am a criminal in the eyes of the law, but I want you to know I am not evil'. In some cases, it may be: 'I may have been like this, but I'm not like that anymore.'
- *To have a chance to explain what happened and why, and answer questions.* When told that the person they have harmed has specific needs, perhaps for an explanation or answers to specific questions, many perpetrators are genuinely moved to respond: 'I want you to know it was not intentional.'
- *To offer help and take steps to sort things out.* Rather than be left with a bad feeling, they can offer and receive reassurance that there won't be repercussions.
- *To atone and find redemption.* Through the courage required to face up to the harm they have caused and take responsibility, they can feel proud, and make their family proud, perhaps for the first time ever. They can regain trust and restore the respect they lost as a result of the crime (including self-respect).
- *To hear how the other person is.* Simple curiosity. This is their story, and yet they only have their half of it. They may be interested in information about the other.

They should be genuine

At the start of the restorative process, 5% motivation is sufficient in the person responsible. However, at the point that they are entering the room for a restorative meeting, they will hopefully be starting to show respect for the other as a person, and participate because they want to help. Although I have quoted stories of successful meetings where the perpetrator's motives have been suspect, there is a danger that if it is simply another criminal justice hoop they are going through, if they don't fully understand what it is about, if they are conditioned to agree to suggestions from professionals without question or if they think it will lead to a lighter punishment, the person they harmed may realise that they are not genuine, and potentially feel yet more aggrieved. The practitioner will always try to assess the perpetrator's authenticity. They will check that their motive is not simply self-serving: an appearance of total self-blame to get others to feel sorry for them, a hard-luck story because they feed off being the 'victim' of circumstances.

It can help to emphasise to the person responsible that while this may be part of their criminal justice programme and they are encouraged to become involved, it is purely for and about mending things between them and the person they harmed. Asking them to reflect back on their understanding of the process and its purpose is a useful check: 'How come you want to meet the person you harmed?'; or 'What do you hope would be the result of a meeting?'

Some may want to make things better, but may simply feel helpless to know what to do. Here, they can be encouraged to believe that a small gesture – an apology, the willingness to hear how someone has been affected, reassurance that it won't happen again – can make a huge difference. Many people harmed by crime, including those most deeply affected, will say that this is all they want. This fact can be presented as good news to the person responsible: they really can do something to help.

Choice and control for those harmed

Restorative justice for those harmed is about choice and control. During the offence (and possibly through the criminal justice process), choice and control were taken away, and they were left frustrated and powerless. Restorative justice is empowering justice, which provides options for involvement to the people who were harmed while giving them a sense of being back in control. For Jo Nodding, who met the man who raped her: "It was about me taking away that control and power from him and getting it back for myself."[7] For Ray Donovan: 'I took control of my life again.... For the first time we were going to get a voice.'[8]

Power is a fluid thing. It is not static and it can shift at any time: through an acknowledgement of responsibility, a disclosure of information, someone standing up for themselves, people rising to the occasion in a restorative process. While the practitioner creates the opportunity and 'facilitates',[9] as far as possible, they also hand the process back to the harmed and the harmer – to those who were involved and those who have been affected.

Keys for the person harmed

Some people harmed by crime know instinctively that the only way to make sense of what happened, to find a way forward, is to meet the person who caused them harm. Ask them what they need and they describe restorative justice. For one woman who had been raped, the idea came to her as a flash of insight. Without knowing that this was even possible, she said: "You know what? I've just had an inspiration. I need to meet him."

If this isn't on offer, some may fight for it. When Claire Chung told a local mediation service that she wanted to meet the person who raped her, the team wrestled with the authorities for two years on her behalf. She told me: "they didn't judge or make assumptions about why on earth I would want to meet the rapist – but did recognise I wouldn't give up!"[10] Without having heard of restorative justice, Jo Berry set about meeting Pat Magee, the man who was responsible for killing her father in the Brighton bomb in 1987. She knew that release and healing could only come from such an encounter.[11]

The need to feel heard

There are many reasons why people harmed choose to engage in restorative justice, some of which are explored in Box 8.4.

Studies indicate that people harmed by crime are no more vindictive than those who haven't been victimised (and are much less punitive than some elements of the media would suggest).[14] In my experience of working with young people who offend, those harmed by their crimes are often much less punitive than could reasonably be expected because, I believe, unlike the public, they *do* have strings attached. The crime put them in a relationship with the person responsible; on that day, their lives became entangled. Relationship brings responsibility, and

Box 8.4: Potential benefits of restorative justice for the person harmed

- *To have a voice.* To feel heard, in a way that eluded them as their case went through the criminal justice system. They may want to speak out, to be acknowledged or for others to recognise the full impact of the offence and the harm that they and their circle have suffered.
- *To receive answers to urgent questions about the crime.* Often, just one person holds that key to questions that have been haunting them. Typical questions include: 'I just want to know why?'; 'Why did you choose me?'; 'Are you sorry?'; 'Are you going to do it again?'
- *To fill in gaps about the incident.* Questions that have been tormenting the person harmed: 'How did you get into the house?'; 'What did you do with my grandmother's engagement ring?'; 'Why did you run away and not help my son, my daughter?' Some questions may appear trivial or irrelevant to everyone else, but unanswered, they may niggle and fester for years. In the most tragic cases, where someone has been killed, it may be information for the relatives about their loved one's dying moments, from the last person to see them alive. Even painful answers can bring some peace. Claire Chung, (mentioned on p 107) explained this to me: "Only the harmer can answer these questions. Without answers, whatever they are, it's just conjecture."
- *To 'face the fear'.* Some sense that the only way to dismiss their demons and so start their recovery is to confront them head-on, that healing may only be possible if they reach out for and connect with the very thing that caused them harm. One woman who had been burgled while she and her children were in the house knew she would have to face fully all of her negative emotions before she could let them go:

  Nights and nights afterwards I was waking up every hour feeling that I wanted to go downstairs and make sure everything is [*sic*] all right, but I didn't want to go downstairs because there may be somebody down there. About six months later he was caught and I was asked if I would like to meet with him. My husband was still very angry and didn't want anything to do with him but that wasn't my view at all and I had to confront what had happened and see this person that has made me so scared.[12]
- *Out of simple curiosity.* 'I want to hear what he has to say for himself.' Some will have received little information from the criminal justice process and will have tried to fill in the missing pieces themselves (often assigning too much blame and responsibility to themselves). They may have been left wondering about the person who caused them harm, unable to create a clear picture of who that person is, what led them to make those choices, what exactly happened. They may be intrigued to hear that this hazy person now wishes to meet them. Or, they may be curious about the process; having been told that a meeting (such

as a Referral Order panel or Restorative Conference) can be set up and they are invited to attend, or that they will have a chance to see inside a prison.

- *To see for themselves if they're sorry and how sincere they are.* They will be the best judge of the other person's attitude and intention and won't be taken in by attempts to appease them.
- *To gain reassurance that it won't happen again – to them or to anyone else.* If they are likely to meet the other person, they may be keen to sort things out, to seek a resolution so that they won't feel awkward or unsafe should they bump into one another in the street.
- *To receive specific reparation, which may be financial.* This is usually lower down the agenda. Most say that a sincere and heartfelt apology – with the reassurance that it won't happen again – is all they wish for: 'An apology would go a long way.' Many will express the hope that the person responsible will learn something from what happened, and in youth justice, they often suggest that the young person undertakes a community reparation activity to help others who are worse off. They want something good to come from a painful experience.
- *To help.* It is tricky for the practitioner when the person harmed says: 'If you think it will do them any good, I will meet them, although I don't need to meet them for myself.' The golden rule in restorative justice is that the 'victim' mustn't be 'used' to benefit the 'offender'. However, if they are freely choosing to engage in the hope that their involvement may make a difference, this is a fine sentiment. A mother met with the woman who had killed her daughter through careless driving in order to relieve the burden she knew that woman would be carrying as a result of causing the accident.[13]
- *To find some meaning and significance in an event that has caused so much distress.* This is a core need for many, and if this can be met by helping the person who harmed them to learn and move on, it can be a powerful motivation for engagement in a restorative meeting.
- *An unusual request.* In one case, a mother of two young boys wanted to ask the young man who burgled her to describe what set him on the path to crime. She wanted to learn what to watch out for so that she could steer her sons along a different path, to a brighter future.

while some will be hoping that the person who harmed them will be hung, drawn and quartered, for many, it is hard to bear responsibility for someone else's suffering, for the thought that another human being (especially when it is a young person) is being punished and imprisoned on their account. They would much prefer something positive and hopeful to come out of the relationship – particularly if they feel that they can use this opportunity to help the person responsible turn their life around. Dave Rogers met the young man who killed his son, Adam, by punching him in the face when Adam was trying to break up a fight:

> Billy forced his way into my life – I didn't ask him to be here but he is and I can't just ignore him or push him back out. I don't want to see another life ruined – it's not too late to turn his life around.[15]

For those harmed, there are many different motivations to take part in restorative justice. Restorative justice offers them meaningful participation in 'their case', and active involvement in what happens next. In their interviews, the practitioner will have heard their story, helped them to identify their needs and explored with them what might make things better.

Blocks for the person harmed

The fact that so many people are willing to take the risk of meeting a person who caused them harm – deliberately, in most cases – is remarkable. Those who decline may simply be too hurt or too fearful. This can be particularly true for younger people, who perhaps haven't built up much resilience against life's knocks. Perhaps they don't want to be recognised for fear of reprisals, or simply worry about feeling uncomfortable or exposed in their neighbourhood. Young people can be deeply affected by a crime, including incidents targeted at others that they happen to witness. An intervention called Protective Behaviours can be an enormous help in their recovery, often giving a young person the courage to take the risk of asking for a restorative meeting (Protective Behaviours is described in the Appendix).

Some people have moved on by the time restorative justice is offered, or consider that things are already sorted to their satisfaction – either by the criminal justice system or through their own initiative. Others have a low opinion of the person who targeted them, and don't believe that the process will do any good, or don't trust their reactions if placed in the same room. Perhaps some don't want to feel better or move on, unconsciously wishing to hold on to their aggrieved status. Unfortunately, for some, the information provided about restorative justice is inadequate for them fully to understand their options and make an informed choice, and, as we saw in Chapter Two, for most, the option simply doesn't exist because so few people who commit crimes are caught.

Sometimes, the person harmed has a suspicion that the service being offered isn't really for them at all. They sense that they are being invited into a process set up for the benefit of the person responsible – or, perhaps, even for the benefit of the practitioner and their agency. It is vital for the practitioner to take the time to really understand what the person who has been harmed needs. Only then can they help them to know for themselves how or why meeting with the person who harmed them might actually meet those needs. If the practitioner gets this right, more people are likely to be willing to engage in the process and meet the individuals who harmed them – because they trust that they really have been understood and that the practitioner isn't offering something for them to opt into to meet their own agenda.

Some people, both those responsible for and those harmed by crime, face resistance from those around them to the suggestion of restorative justice. Perhaps wanting to protect their friend or relative, and fearing that it could make things worse, they try to persuade them against the idea – and are sometimes vehemently opposed. It may be that this is a knee-jerk reaction to the thought of time and attention being given to the 'other side', and it could be based on some ignorance of the process and its potential benefit. In Claire Chung's experience, other people continually make judgement values for both the person responsible and the person harmed, leading to a further feelings of loss of control and disempowerment.[16]

The end of the journey

The reality, though, is that many people choose not to be involved, no matter how fine the approach. If either party is clearly indicating that they do not wish to engage in a restorative process, the practitioner must accept this. They must honour their decision and not deem it a failure if there is no meeting. The best process and outcome in any situation is the one decided by those involved, and as professionals, we must try to hide our disappointment.

People harmed who say 'no' can still be offered support, kept updated on the perpetrator's case and be signposted to other agencies as appropriate – and, if possible, be given the choice to opt in at a later date if they change their mind.

It is sometimes possible to salvage a little restorative spark at the end of this kind of conversation. The practitioner can ask whether the speaker has any message that they would like to pass on to the other person. This may simply be that it is over and there are no hard feelings. If it is the person harmed, would they like the person responsible to know how they have been affected? This real-life information can still be an invaluable resource for their case manager to challenge defensive thinking and false assumptions as part of a victim awareness or offending behaviour programme.

Notes

[1] Walgrave, L. (2003) 'Imposing restoratation instead of inflicting pain', in A. von Hirsch, J. Roberts, A.E. Bottoms, K. Roach, and M. Schiff (eds) *Restorative justice: Competing or reconcilable paradigms?*, Oxford: Hart Publishers, p 62.

[2] Walgrave, L. (2007) 'Integrating criminal justice and restorative justice', in G. Johnson and D. Van Ness (eds) *Handbook of restorative justice*, Cullumpton, Devon: Willan, p 560.

[3] Braithwaite, J. (1989) *Crime, shame and reintegration*, Cambridge: Cambridge University Press.

[4] Crawford, A. and Newburn, T. (2003) *Youth offending and restorative justice*, Cullompton: Willan Publishing.

[5] Zehr, H. (2002) *The little book of restorative justice*, Intercourse, PA: Good Books, p 19.

[6] Woolf, P. (2008) *The damage done*, London: Bantam Books, p 300.

[7] Jo spoke to BBC Radio Tees, available as an RJC (Restorative Justice Council) website resource at: www.restorativejustice.org.uk/?p=resources&search=jo +nodding (see also Video Resources in the Appendix).

[8] Ray and Vi Donovan's story is available online at: www.chrisdonovantrust. org/

[9] The word 'facilitate' means both to 'help forward an action or a process', and to 'assist the progress of a person' (http://dictionary.reference.com), both of which neatly sum up the facilitator's task, which, as far as possible, is to hand control back to those whose process it is.

[10] Claire's story is available at www.telegraph.co.uk/news/uknews/ crime/8378549/Dr-Claire-Chung-has-a-right-to-be-angry.html and at www.telegraph.co.uk/news/uknews/crime/9716234/Why-I-must-speak-out-to-stop-my-rapist-being-freed.html

[11.] Jo and Pat's story can be found on Jo's website (www.buildingbridgesforpeace. org).

[12.] 'Behind the Hoodie' (https://vimeo.com/23797353).

[13.] Barbara Tonge, writing in *The Friend*, 9 March 2012.

[14.] Wood, J. and Tendayi Viki, G. (2004) 'Public perceptions of crime and punishment', in J. Adler (ed) *Forensic psychology: Concepts, debates and practice*, Cullompton: Willan, p 23.

[15.] Eva Simpson (2012) 'A father meets his son's killer', *Life* supplement, *The Times*, 20 August.

[16.] See note 10 for Claire's story.

Part Four
Empathy Level Three: hearing

'Everyone is different and, obviously, there has to be a willingness from both sides — but it can be a hugely beneficial experience…. He was not a scary sight, just a human being sitting at a table, waiting, anxious.'

(Katja Rosemberg)[1]

CHAPTER NINE

Indirect restorative justice

The practitioner has now met both sides separately, has heard their stories and explored their needs and wishes. They are in the extraordinary position of being the only person to have the whole picture, to have heard people's different perspectives on the same event. They may know information about one side that could be of enormous import and benefit to the other.

If insights and needs have been expressed that would be helpful for the other person to know, the practitioner may ask permission to share snippets of information between people. In this stage of the restorative process, the practitioner moves between the parties, drip-feeding information to each side. They may share a little about the other person's perspective, paint a picture of what they are like, describe their attitude. They may share information about the impact of the crime, how the other person is now faring, what the person is telling them about their needs and what would help the person to move forward.

Some practitioners write down the information and agree it with the person who is sharing it, to make sure that they have not introduced their own thoughts or feelings, and to be clear that they have permission to pass it on. It is not uncommon for people to start the restorative process off with written correspondence, perhaps expressing why they would like to meet the other, establishing some basic information in advance of a face-to face–encounter. Stephen, one of the young men who met with Ray and Vi Donovan, describes this stage of the process:

> During the preparation meetings we exchanged messages and I knew some of the things that they had questions about before the face to face contact. One of the things they wanted me to know before we met, was that they felt no anger, and this really helped me to relax and prepare to face them. I too was able to pass on to them that I wanted them to feel free to ask anything.[2]

Care with the ownership of information

Knowledge is power, and the practitioner must take great care with the ownership of information. Once disclosed, it can't be retracted,

Cartoon 9.1: Personal information must only be shared with explicit permission...

and personal information must only be shared between parties with explicit permission.

This preparation stage of indirect communication can help to close the gap. However, there is still a gap with indirect restorative work. So much of our communication is non-verbal; so much of the information we glean from others is subliminal. People communicating indirectly may 'hear', but they won't see, the other, and are left with a two-dimensional image. Remote evidence is less restorative. A distraught young man said: "I wish they would understand that I'm really not a yob!" He'll have a hard time convincing the people he offended against unless they meet in person, get a chance to really judge his sincerity, see his expression and hear the regret in his voice. Creative use of audio or video technology can work well if people won't or can't meet in person, and videoconferencing has been used successfully to bridge the gap across continents.

Indirect communication

For many people, indirect communication is as far as they can go (see Figure 9.1). The gap is reduced but won't be fully closed. There is an interesting debate about whether a 'direct' restorative process where people meet face to face is 'better' than one involving 'indirect' communication, through letters, videos, gifts, financial compensation or messages via a third party. There is no doubt that a face-to-face meeting is potentially more powerful than an exchange of information or letters. However, it is dangerous to conclude that direct restorative justice is a 'better' outcome. If the practitioner remains neutral and impartial (and therefore disinterested in achieving any particular outcome), what will come out of the process will be the best fit for that particular unique set of circumstances and the individuals involved.

Figure 9.1: Indirect communication increases insight and empathy: the two parties are mirroring one another, moving up the empathy scale by sharing information and narrowing the gap between them

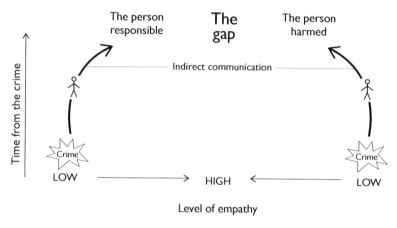

The period of indirect communication may be the end of the restorative journey – or it may become the assessment and preparation process for a restorative meeting. If the parties wish to meet, careful assessment and preparation will ensure that the encounter is physically and emotionally safe for the participants. Where there is a wider gap, a deeper empathetic divide, where people's stories don't quite match or there is disputed harm or shared responsibility, and particularly in the more serious and complex cases, meticulous assessment and preparation are crucial. In cases of rape and murder, this part of the journey can take years.

Why so little restorative justice?

Although mentioned in legislation, with encouragement for local authorities and criminal justice agencies to provide restorative justice services, the reality on the ground is that restorative justice is patchy and many areas struggle or fail to deliver. We saw in Chapter Four that there are interesting debates and attempts to bring more restorative justice into criminal justice at different stages, and the level of restorative rhetoric is increasing, but the large majority of people responsible for or harmed by crime are still not offered the option of restorative justice.[3] Even where there are services that are adequately funded, many practitioners find it difficult to find clients who will engage, and complain about low take-up.

Although the figure is rising, in 2011, the Restorative Justice Council estimated that only one in 100 victims are offered restorative justice.[4] Before you even get started, the person responsible is known only in a minority of cases. There also has to be a local restorative justice service with the resources and information to contact everyone involved. Some services automatically exclude certain categories of crime (such as domestic violence, murder, manslaughter, sexual offences or hate crime), even if people involved in those offences might be wishing to meet. It may be that the person who was harmed can't be traced, having moved or changed their phone number.

Another built-in factor that leads to an attrition in the number of potential restorative justice processes, and, in particular, in the number of direct face-to-face meetings, is the simple fact that it isn't enough to have one party keen, willing, able (and appropriate) to be involved; any restorative communication requires at least two people.[5]

It is frustrating and painful for the restorative practitioner if one side is ready and keen for a meeting and the other is not (see Figure 9.2). They may find that the person who caused harm is deeply remorseful, ready to do anything to make amends, but with nowhere for that yearning to go. Conversely, the person harmed may be hurting deeply and desperate for reassurance and answers, only to find that they face a defensive wall that cannot be breached. In the case of Damilola Taylor, his father Richard wants to reach out to understand, help and forgive his son's attackers, but is prevented (see Box 9.1). If one is open to the process, but the other is closed, knowing how powerful and beneficial a meeting can be, there is a danger that the practitioner may try too hard to encourage the unwilling party in these circumstances, perhaps rising too far up the 'continuum of voluntariness', as described in Chapter Eight, to coerce or even force engagement – with potentially disastrous results.

Cartoon 9.2: Any restorative communication requires at least two people

Box 9.1: Extract from an interview with Damilola Taylor's father

Mr Taylor, a retired civil servant awarded an OBE in 2010 for "services to the prevention of youth violence" cuts a picture of dignified anguish, and admits he still wrestles with horrendous feelings of "anger, bitterness and yes, revenge." But when you ask him if he could ever forgive the Preddie brothers, who were 12 and 13 when they stabbed Damilola with a broken bottle on a Peckham estate, his line softens unexpectedly. "If they had used prison to reform themselves instead of just getting bigger in the gym, if they had apologised to me and my family instead of bragging about how tough they are, I would have embraced them. I would have hugged my son's killers. If they had shown proper remorse, that would have warranted me to forgive them, to talk about turning their lives round, and it would have freed me to move on too. This was a big opportunity missed. I am not blaming the prison system because some people come out reformed, but these brothers have never apologised. So my bitterness is not only that Dam died, that my wife Gloria died four years ago because of a heart attack brought on by the stress of his death, but also that they have not shown a shred of remorse."[6]

Figure 9.2: It is frustrating when one side is ready and the other is not

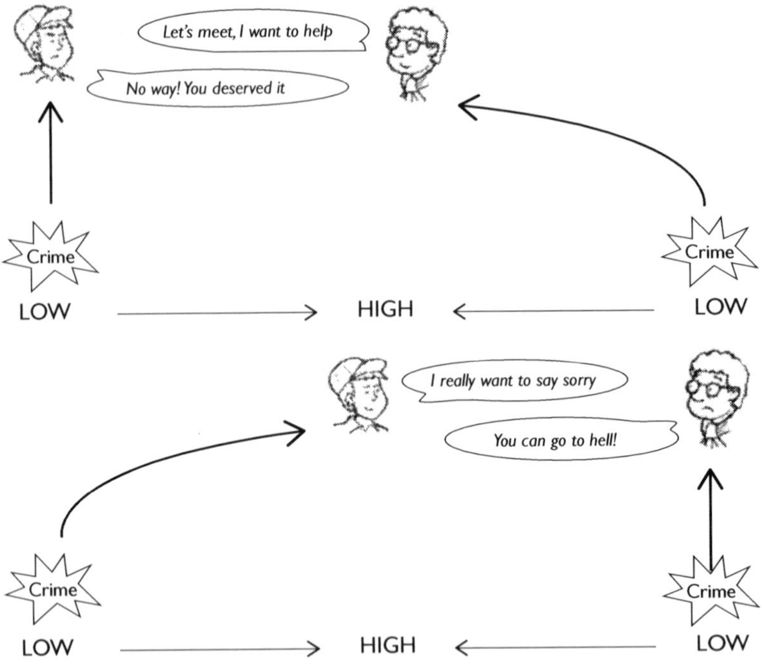

A partnership of the willing

Imagine a practitioner holding nine cases involving nine different crimes, with each case comprising someone responsible for and someone harmed by that offence. Those nine cases will involve 18 people in all. If three of the people harmed are up for a face-to-face meeting, another three only wish to communicate indirectly and the final three aren't interested in or willing to engage in any form of restorative justice process, and the same level of interest holds for all those responsible, there are nine potential permutations (see Table 9.1).

From this hypothetical group, although a third of the 18 people involved are wishing for a face-to-face restorative meeting, in only one in every nine cases will that be possible, with a further three leading to some form of indirect restorative contact. Put another way, a restorative justice service where only 11% of their caseload end up with a restorative meeting might feel that they are doing something wrong. However, to reach that figure, as Table 9.1 indicates, fully 66% could have been wishing for some form of restorative communication, with 33% wanting to meet the other person in a face-to-face meeting, many of whom will be frustrated by the unwillingness of the other side.

Table 9.1: The attritional affect of needing a partnership of the willing

Persons responsible	Persons harmed	Outcome
1. Not interested	1. Not interested	No restorative justice
2. Only interested in indirect	2. Not interested	No restorative justice
3. Wishing for face-to-face	3. Not interested	No restorative justice
4. Not interested	4. Only interested in indirect	No restorative justice
5. Only interested in indirect	5. Only interested in indirect	Indirect restorative justice
6. Wishing for face-to-face	6. Only interested in indirect	Indirect restorative justice
7. Not interested	7. Wishing for face-to-face	No restorative justice
8. Only interested in indirect	8. Wishing for face-to-face	Indirect restorative justice
9. Wishing for face-to-face	9. Wishing for face-to-face	**A restorative meeting**

Despite the attritional effect and the need for a partnership of the willing, some areas manage to claim that up to 70% of cases coming from court lead to some form of direct or indirect restorative process (although there is considerable variation in what is recorded as 'restorative'[7]). Other areas have almost none, which would suggest that the problem is not that people aren't interested, but may instead be one of finding the right approach or invitation, the right 'key', to overcome any potential blocks and encourage involvement.

This is borne out by research into Restorative Cautions in the Thames Valley.[8] During the period studied, the majority of crime victims opted out of involvement in restorative justice, leading to disappointing take-up figures. When they were approached in follow-up interviews, it emerged that they had little understanding of what they were rejecting. When the restorative process was clarified, over half said that they would probably have attended had they been given better information. The quality of the approach from the practitioner is crucial in enabling people to have confidence that restorative justice will meet their needs.[9] Receiving a letter or a form with a tick box may apparently offer people lots of 'choice', but experience shows that meeting both parties in person results in more restorative justice.

Notes

[1] Katja Rosemberg, who met the man who raped her (he was 16 at the time), speaking about her experience of a restorative meeting, quoted in *I Magazine*, 11 January 2014, p 15.

[2] Extract from a letter written by Stephen, one of the young men who murdered Christopher Donovan, quoted in 'Restorative justice – what it meant to me' (www.chrisdonovantrust.org/restorative-justice.php).

3. The new Code of Practice for Victims of Crime indicates the strengthening commitment of the government to restorative justice – and how far there is still to go. In contrast to the 2006 Code, in which restorative justice with adult offenders wasn't mentioned and Youth Offending Teams were instructed to 'Decide if it would be appropriate to invite the victim to become involved in a restorative justice intervention – dependant on provision', the 2013 Code *entitles* the victim of both adult and young offenders to 'Receive information about Restorative Justice and how you can take part', although still adding: 'This is dependent on the provision of Restorative Justice in your local area' (www.gov.uk/government/uploads/system/uploads/attachment_data/file/254459/code-of-practice-victims-of-crime.pdf).

4. Restorative Justice Council (2011) 'A new way of doing justice: response to the Sentencing Green Paper, *Breaking the cycle*', March (www.restorativejustice.org.uk/?p=resources&search=&id=&sort=az&author=&keyword=27).

5. Some services use the term 'restorative justice' for interventions, such as victim empathy work or 'restorative clinics', that involve no communication between the two parties involved in an offence. The definition used here would stipulate that without that communication, the encounter isn't 'restorative'.

6. Richard Taylor, speaking to the *Evening Standard*, 25 January 2012.

7. The Criminal Justice Inspection Northern Ireland report on youth restorative conferencing in Northern Ireland stated that a 'victim' was present in 67% of 775 conferences held in 2006: 38% were personal victims of the crime; 28% were victim representatives (usually representatives of corporate or public bodies); 28% were 'general victims' providing a broad view on the impact of an offence that had no victim; and 6% were representatives of communities harmed by the offence. Criminal Justice Inspection Northern Ireland (2008) *Youth Conference Service: Inspection of the Youth Conference Service in Northern Ireland*, Belfast: CJNI.

8. Hoyle, C., Young, R. and Hill, R. (2002) *Proceed with caution: An evaluation of the Thames Valley Police initiative in restorative cautioning*, York: Joseph Rowntree Foundation.

9. See Restorative Justice Council (2014) *How to engage victims in a restorative process*, London: Restorative Justice Council.

CHAPTER TEN

The restorative meeting

A restorative meeting brings those responsible for a crime and those they have harmed together in the same room. One of the reasons why practitioners get excited about restorative meetings is their relative rarity, the number of restorative meetings always appearing to be disappointingly low in the statistics. As we have seen in previous chapters, there are many 'exit routes' before restorative justice can even be considered, which are summed up in Figure 10.1.

Figure 10.1: Exit routes – the points along the road when the potential for a restorative meeting can fall off the agenda

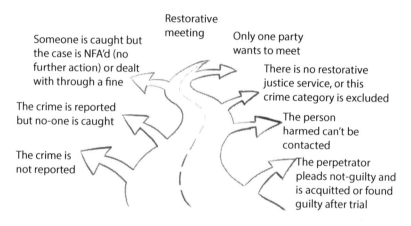

The timing has to be right. Different people have different timescales, which can be tricky if one side is ready and the other requires more time and preparation; someone will have to be patient. Often, the window of opportunity, before people lose interest or talk themselves out of involvement, is brief. The practitioner will aim not to be the cause of any delay themselves, and be aware that the impact of information and the insight it offers fades with time.

There are then the logistics of making arrangements so that everyone can attend. Some restorative meetings can be brought together in a matter of days. More usually, it will take two or three months from making initial contact with the parties to welcoming everyone at the start of a restorative meeting, especially if many people have been affected or if the person responsible is in prison. Each person will have been met by the practitioner at least two or three times as they shuttle between everyone, carrying messages and impressions. In serious cases requiring significant preparation, it may be years before everyone is in the same room.

Restorative meetings are tricky affairs to organise, with frequent false starts, and even the best-laid plans go awry. After all the preparation, it is not uncommon for someone to pull out at the last minute – or simply fail to turn up on the day. The practitioner will have warned both sides that this could happen, but, even so, it is a major blow all round.

Whether it is days or years, coming to a restorative meeting, reaching the point where everyone is in the same room, is little short of a triumph for the practitioner. In many ways, once everyone is sitting down, the hardest part is already over.

The start of the restorative meeting

With the exception of those in prison, restorative meetings are held at a neutral venue – a community centre, youth club or library – with everyone seated in a circle. The practitioner will have thought carefully about the venue, visited in advance, considered the layout of the room, planned the position of the chairs (who will sit next to whom, who might need to make a quick exit, how to avoid symbolically trapping the person harmed, etc), and arranged for a spare room if people need time out – not to mention car parking, arrival times and refreshments. If the meeting is in a prison, the practitioner may offer to show those harmed around in advance so that they can feel more comfortable on the day.

The practitioner will update their risk assessment to ensure that the meeting is as safe as possible, while recognising that there will always be an element of risk and it is not in their gift to promise absolute safety. Safety has to be shared, and while the practitioner will have assessed everyone's ability to manage their behaviour, a restorative meeting is a leap of faith for the practitioner as well as for the participants. I remember asking a woman who was about to meet the person who had mugged her, leaving her with permanent injuries, whether she wanted tea or coffee to be on offer. She said "better not", that she didn't trust herself not to throw her cup at the person whom she was about to meet. Plastic cups and water were provided. By the end of the meeting she was holding hands with the person responsible for causing her so much distress, and recognizing that he was also suffering, she expressed a sincere wish for him to have a good life, to be happy. No one could have anticipated that level of movement in advance, least of all the participants.

Although, for simplicity, this book is written as if there is just one facilitator, there are usually two. Co-facilitation has a number of benefits, including managing arrivals and departures, coping with unexpected crises, ensuring that no one is left alone if someone needs time out, supporting best practice, and encouraging reflection.[1] The practitioner's task will now be to use skilful means to manage the meeting and create an ambiance that will maximise the potential benefit for everyone. The Restorative Justice Council practitioner registration stipulates a minimum 20 hours of initial training, during which they learn, practise and internalise the restorative themes, restorative language and restorative techniques. They can use these freely, facilitating the meeting more tightly when 'scaffolding' is required to make it safe, loosening their control when participants are engaging constructively, gently bringing people back to the ground rules when this is required. Throughout the process, the practitioner will model responsibility, honesty, interest and respect – and in doing so, expect the same of the participants. They remain present and alert, listening carefully to everyone's contributions without judgement or reaction, allowing space for people to explore issues and express themselves fully. The practitioner will exude confidence and serenity even if they too are nervous, which is deeply reassuring for everyone.

Unless the chairs are bolted to the floor (sometimes the case in prisons), restorative meetings are arranged with the chairs in a circle, with either a low table for flowers and drinks or no table at all. There are practical benefits to this arrangement. When sitting in a circle, everyone is clearly visible and can make eye contact with everyone else. There is no one to hide behind, no way to block someone out. Each person shares an equal position and equal status with everyone else, and there is no 'head of the table'. Circles are naturally inclusive, and everyone sitting in the circle knows that their presence is important, and that having a place in the circle confers a sense of belonging. This, after all, is their crime, their business.

During the meeting, the circle becomes a container for everyone's stories: their thoughts and feelings, their confidences, their hopes and wishes for the future. Beyond the benefits for any group process, circles have their own inherent power dynamic. They bring a sense of balance and wholeness. They have no start or finish, and when a thought or theme goes round the circle, energy can flow perpetually. It is not surprising that the circle is a powerful and sacred symbol for many of the world's religions, and that for aboriginal societies, working in circles is the natural process for activities involving relationship-building and conflict resolution.

The stage is now set. A restorative meeting is a potent encounter, and in creating the circle, the practitioner sets the scene for the container to become a crucible for restorative alchemy (people who have themselves been through a restorative process say that this phrase accurately describes their experience). The restorative circle has a power that can transform a conflict, often far beyond the expectations of participants and practitioners; a power to turn a harmful and negative situation into an opportunity for reconciliation and healing. Joanna Nodding, who met the man who raped her, said: "It allowed me to have the opportunity of a life-changing experience."[2]

At the start of the meeting, everyone is nervous and uncomfortable (see Figure 10.2). People may physically shake. It is not unusual for one or the other to need extra time in the car park or a reception room to summon their courage, and it is helpful if they have supporters to offer encouragement and reassurance. Not quite knowing what is coming, and in some cases genuinely expecting to be shouted at, punched, have water thrown over them or worse, they naturally enter the room fairly low down the empathy scale. They may arrive assuming the worst of the other, anticipating that their preconceptions and stereotypes will be confirmed – even if the practitioner has previously assured them otherwise. Comments like 'I can't believe that they didn't yell at me' or 'I expected her to punch me' are not uncommon. A young man who met with the woman who's house he burgled said: 'When

Figure 10.2: Although the physical gap between the parties closes as the meeting is about to start, with people feeling nervous, they can potentially slip lower down the empathy scale

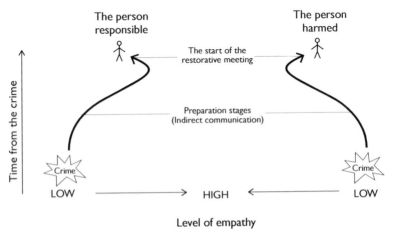

I was actually told a day and I knew she was going to be there, I was constantly worried that she was going to jump up and start hitting me, screaming at me and I didn't know what to expect at all.'[3] There is a danger at this point that signals will be missed, that behaviour will be misinterpreted. If the person responsible is laughing, can't string a sentence together or stares at the ground or out of the window, this is more likely to be through nerves than because he or she doesn't care.

Often in life, the anticipation is worse than the thing itself. The person walking down the corridor towards a meeting with the person who harmed them or whom they harmed will be full of alertness, full of expectation, with a very hazy idea of what to expect. It can be a relief to enter the room, to finally see the person there, the physical body in the room. Everything changes, something is contained.

Lots will be going on in the first few seconds and minutes of the meeting, everyone's senses fully engaged, subtle communication starting at all levels, including much that is out of awareness. The shift in perception can be seismic; Ginnie Fourie, whose daughter was killed in the 1993 Heidelburg Tavern Massacre in Cape Town, South Africa said: "In that moment, I saw remorse in his eyes and body language. It would have been so much easier if he'd been a monster with horns and a tail – if there was someone to hate."[4] In Chapter Four, I mentioned a young man who had described lying awake in his prison cell at night thinking about how he wanted to harm the woman he had robbed for getting him 'sent down'. When she entered the room at the start of the restorative meeting, he said that any residual rage and anger disappeared. This was only the second time he had ever met her, and the first time he had held a knife to her throat.

It takes courage for anyone who has been deeply hurt to choose to meet their tormentor in person, but it usually pays off. For those who have had little or no information about the person who harmed them, they may have mentally filled in the gaps, constructed a frightening image of their tormentor. They may have extrapolated their fear of their unknown attacker into fear of everyone unknown. In the cold light of day, the person in the chair opposite is less scary, and, in fact, is clearly just as nervous as they are – if not more so. The burglar isn't a mad axe-wielding murderer, but a young lad who crawled in through a tiny skylight. The man who wielded a broken bottle is sober and reflective and sitting next to his mum. Goode describes this moment; 'The most important effect for us all was, I suspect, that we were able to move forward from our fantasies. The imaginary picture we had of the man who had invaded our home was undermined by the well-dressed, calm, articulate person in front of us.'[5] To find out that this person has a mum, a dad, children and a job can be a revelation. For the person harmed, what happened was out of their control, and now here they are, back in control. The demon has gone: a frail, flawed and often frightened human being in their place.

Cartoon 10.1: Anticipation is worse than the reality

It takes courage for the perpetrator too – they tend not to be cold, heartless beasts devoid of feelings and without fear. Reggie Aitchison talks about the moment he met Kathleen, whose house he broke into:

> I was full of fear about meeting you. I thought 'how's she going to react?', but felt you deserved an explanation, and deserved to get how you felt across to me as well. The way I see it is that you must have imagined some kind of monster going through your stuff.[6]

Hearing the story of the person responsible

The practitioner's challenge now is to provide the conditions where the parties feel safe enough to shift from their starting positions. While people naturally arrive feeling anxious, wary and defensive, in order to move, they must open up sufficiently to change from wanting to persuade the other of their own perspective to being open to fully hearing another perspective. This is usually not possible until they themselves feel heard. Movement comes from insight, which can come through words, actions or appearances, including the whole range of non-verbal communication.

The practitioner welcomes everyone into the circle. Housekeeping issues are mentioned, and it is important for people to feel that they can take a break if they need 'time out'. The practitioner may offer or elicit suggestions about how the meeting can run as smoothly as possible. These typically include something about listening and not interrupting when someone else is talking, respectful language and behaviour, perhaps a mention of talking honestly and being gentle with one another, and something about confidentiality. The practitioner will establish clearly the focus and context of the meeting, reminding participants about how it relates to any criminal justice processes: 'We are here to talk about the burglary that John committed on the 24th of November last year, for which he received a 12-month community sentence.'

During the first stage of the meeting, the focus is the past, looking back over the events that led up to the crime, and thinking about everything that has happened since. The practitioner encourages everyone present to share their story in turn, asking the same questions and building on the same themes that were used during the initial meetings with each participant.

Kay Pranis has written powerfully about the crucial role of storytelling process and life narrative in restorative justice:

> Personal narratives are the primary source of information and wisdom in restorative justice approaches. ...The critical element is the use of personal narratives to understand the harms, the needs, the pains and the capacities of all participants so that an appropriate new story can be constructed. Personal stories allow people to engage emotional and spiritual components of their being as well as the physical and mental. In restorative approaches storytelling is often an iterative process – the story is told many different times as understandings are increased and greater and greater depths of communication become possible.[7]

The stories start with the person responsible. This may feel counter-intuitive, but it usually works best. If the person harmed were asked to speak first, the person responsible could find it difficult to listen properly, worrying about what they are going to say when it comes to their turn to speak (unlike the person harmed, who has come specifically to hear their account). They might feel defensive, on the alert for any aspects of the story being shared by the person they harmed that they disagree with, or which places them in a poor light. If they are the first to speak, however, they are invited to put more of themselves into the meeting and it allows them to take responsibility from the outset. Meanwhile the person they harmed won't be put in the spotlight from the start and can settle into the meeting, get a sense of the person who harmed them and decide how much they feel comfortable sharing. Although this is a generalisation, the difference illustrates the differing motivations for attending; the person responsible needing to get something off their chest, the person harmed needing answers.

The person responsible will be carefully led by the practitioner in talking about what happened. When they have described the offence in their own words, they will be invited to go back and explore their thoughts and feelings at critical moments in their narrative, the practitioner asking the open questions of the restorative enquiry: 'What happened?'; 'What were you thinking?'; 'What did you feel?' By zooming in on what someone was thinking and feeling at precise moments in time, a much rounder picture of the crime emerges than the one that may have been heard in court: 'What were you thinking when you first saw the open bathroom window?'; 'How were you feeling at that moment?'; 'At the point you were climbing in through the window?'; 'When you realised that someone was in the house?'; 'When you were running down the street with just a half-full bottle of aftershave?';'When the police knocked on your door at six o'clock in the morning?';'In the police cells?';'Looking back on it all now?' These questions were rehearsed during preparation, and knowing the questions that are coming provides the person responsible with the necessary confidence to move forward.

Practitioners have to put themselves aside during the meeting, taking care not to fill the silences. An awkward gap often leads to new insights, deeper sharing. They try not to tell participants what they were feeling, avoid answering their own questions or putting words into people's mouths. However, if someone is struggling, or a key point is overlooked, the practitioner may nudge them to see if they wish to share information that was mentioned during preparation. In doing so, they will be careful not to take over or intrude too much into the meeting, respecting that there are certain things that the participant may decide not to disclose at this point. They may check with the person harmed to ensure that everything they need to know about the crime is explored. Now is the time for those unanswered questions: 'How did you get in?';'How did you find the money under the lining paper in my drawer?';'What happened to my wallet?';'Did I do something to offend you?' A chip shop owner gave chase to a youth who ran off with a can of coke without paying and who then turned on him with a knife. He wanted to know whether the young man would have used the knife if he hadn't backed down (he said he would).

Cartoon 10.2: Hey – your burden looks familiar somehow

Hearing the perpetrator's explanation often leads to revelations for those harmed. As the story unfolds, they are drawn into their chaotic, broken and often cruel world, and may start to realise not only that the person who caused them harm is also affected by what happened, but that the offence arose from an experience of unhappiness, suffering and loss that goes a long way back – perhaps to their childhood. The practitioner may gently encourage the person responsible to tease out this 'back story' to the crime, perhaps inviting them to put a finger on 'when this all started'. For that person to make the changes required to desist from future offending, they will not only need to accept the consequences of their past actions, but also be challenged to shift the beliefs that underpin them.

Kathleen found answers to the 'Why?' question when Reggie, who had burgled her, told his story: 'I didn't know you were on drugs and I didn't know your tale until it all came out. You were a different lad altogether. You weren't the same Reggie that I'd seen dart out of my house.'[8] Sometimes, those details are desperately poignant. I have mentioned Peter Woolf, who has written about his meeting with Will Riley in *The damage done*. Peter shares an early memory of being in a pram with a baby bottle full of Guinness 'to shut me up'. At the point that he broke into Will's house and assaulted him, his life had become an endless cycle of drugs, violence and prison, to the point where he was eating whatever food he could find on the pavement and living, literally, in a rubbish bin.[9]

Details of a path of past unhappiness leading up to the offence may not come to light. Often, the practitioner knows the details (from police, probation and Crown Prosecution Service reports, and from discussions during preparation meetings) and may be biting their tongue, dying to share information in the meeting, knowing that it would answer the 'Why?' question, but also knowing that the person responsible must choose for themselves what they feel comfortable disclosing. If a detailed picture doesn't emerge, there may be snippets of information, a general sense from the demeanour of the perpetrator or hints, for example, when a young teenager turns up with a care worker instead of a parent, or an adult clearly has no one who comes to visit them in prison.

Perhaps there hasn't been previous suffering. Empathy can still be unlocked for those harmed. The person sitting opposite may be surprisingly young, clearly socially inadequate or unwell. If the meeting is held in a prison, those harmed will see the living conditions first-hand.

It may also be evident that the person who caused harm is suffering now, here in the restorative meeting. They may be struggling with nerves and acutely uncomfortable, or expressing disgust at their own behaviour. A young man who got caught up with a group attacking an elderly gentleman walked into his restorative meeting, his hat pulled down low, his face bright red and his eyes averted. Before he had even managed to sit down, he blurted out "I am so sorry for what I did." If the person responsible is apologetic and contrite, that helps enormously (while any display of a lack of remorse, lack of interest, insincerity or attitude will send empathy plummeting).

It is harder to dislike or hate someone who is suffering. This first part of the restorative meeting can expose the fact that everyone is unhappy. If the person harmed has been stuck in their own suffering, suddenly seeing the suffering of the person who caused them harm can be a release. Claire Chung reached an understanding of the man who raped her when he said that he had already been identified as a 'sex pest' at 11. She saw the destruction caused when his mother left the family when he was a child, the danger of labelling, the lack of appropriate help, 'the cycle of damage that the offender was actively engaged in perpetuating'.[10]

Hearing the story of the person harmed

In preparatory meetings, the practitioner will have clarified with the person harmed how deeply they want to enter their story – whether they wish to go into every detail or just bring out the essentials of the traumatic event. As they share their side of the story, strong feelings may arise. It's natural if anger and rage flare up in face of the abuse, disrespect and hurt that they experienced through the actions of the person sitting opposite. Anger can be cathartic, cleansing and healing. Reflecting afterwards, Kathleen, who met the man who had burgled her house, said:

> When I [met] you there was still built-up anger, and when we got talking I burst out in tears. All that hatred had built up that much, that's how I released it. And [after that] I just built my life back up. All the hatred and everything went out. It was a relief.[11]

Now, it is time for the person responsible to hear about the damage they have caused. This can be tough. As details emerge of fear, anxiety, sleepless nights, financial loss, shattered confidence, hospital treatment – perhaps an anxious parent or spouse waiting outside the operating theatre door – it is common to see the colour rise in their neck and face. They may go still and stiff and look deeply uncomfortable as they sit through waves of emotion: of distress, rage, bitterness and anger, with a hearty condemnation of their bad choices and harmful actions. Watching the guilt and discomfort increase as the person responsible hears the other side of their story unfolding directly from the person they have harmed, the practitioner may be holding their breath, willing them to have the courage to see the process through. They may need to check that they are good to continue, or choose to suggest a break. Sometimes, this sharing precipitates a crisis in the meeting, where one party or the other bursts into tears, has to leave the room to compose themselves and shows their courage by returning. This can help the empathy shift, eliciting a compassionate response from other participants.

The simple fact that the person who harmed them is listening can shift things for the person harmed, can be seen as an expression of remorse. Coming through to the other side, they will sometimes acknowledge that they needed to express their feelings, to vent their anger. At this point, they may see the person responsible as if for the first time, notice their discomfort and realise what it will have been like for them on the receiving end, perhaps reaching out at this point: 'Thank you for hearing that'; 'I needed to get that off my chest, and now that I have I can put this behind me, with no hard feelings between us'; 'I was surprised that you had the guts to come – I really didn't think you would.' In one meeting, a young man who had seriously hurt a woman had to take a break and leave the room before she had finished telling her story – he couldn't stay sitting, listening to the distress and anger he'd caused. When he came back in, she had completely changed, her anger gone, and she said: "I'm really proud of you for coming to this meeting today."

Often, a key piece of information about harm caused can go deep for the person responsible: they hadn't thought about the four-year-old child living in the house they burgled, and feel gutted to hear that he or she is still asking: 'When are the burglars coming back?' They're uncomfortable that the person they robbed still feels unsafe, is constantly looking over their shoulder, has moved house because of what happened. They couldn't have guessed that the car they stole (because it was old and easy to break into) was, in fact, the only item left from its owner's father, who has passed away.

Peter Woolf describes what happened as the details emerged of the havoc that he had caused through his burglaries: from Will Riley, whose young daughter saw him covered in blood being taken away in an ambulance, and from a doctor, whose research materials and patient notes – his life's work – had been lost with the laptop that Peter sold on for a £20 wrap of heroin:

> My throat closed. I couldn't speak; I felt I couldn't breathe. It was like I was squashed into a tiny space. I felt suddenly very hot, and then very cold. Tears rushed into my eyes. And something else happened, too. There was no longer a devil taunting me, tempting me; instead, someone invisible stepped forward and slid a sharp cold blade deep between my ribs and into my heart. I had no answers for how I had ruined these people's lives ... I'd known this before, but now, for the very first time in my life, I felt it. And it hurt.[12]

The practitioner can't prescribe or control the arising of guilt or the shift towards empathy; it has to happen spontaneously, if at all. What they can do is to establish the expectation that people will listen respectfully to one another without interruption. They can encourage honesty.

Differences between the two accounts of what happened, disputes over 'facts', which have the potential to derail the conversation into a tit-for-tat fight over detail, often melt away. A gentle discipline grows in the room, where people don't feel a need to challenge or disagree with the other to reinforce a position, or persuade them of their own perspective. Knowing that they will have their own turn to be heard enables people to relax, and having space to have their say releases them to see and hear the other perspective. When we are talking, we can't really listen, and if we are really listening, we can't also talk.

The truth will out

One of the key features of restorative practice that separates it from the rest of criminal justice is that the practitioner remains non-aligned, neutral, spared from any duty to judge. Wrong actions may be condemned by the participants themselves, either by the person responsible – 'It shouldn't have happened', 'I should have walked away', 'I did the wrong thing' – or by those they harmed. Often, judgement is implicit rather than explicit, and while not condoning harmful deeds, as stories unfold, people may start to understand how those harmful events came about.

Restorative meetings become self-policing. Bullshit is quickly exposed and challenged, sometimes verbally, sometimes with a look that says 'Yeah, right' more loudly than words: 'I hadn't planned to steal a car, I just "happened" to try the door and found it open'; 'It was my mate's idea, I didn't want to be kicking you and stamping on your head'; 'I was intending to give you your phone back.' Claire Chung[13] calls this 'a real-time challenging of explanations'. Reminders of the ground rules are expressed by participants, and as the process unfolds, the natural and intrinsic power and logic of restorative justice spontaneously takes over. In fact, sometimes, one or other participant (usually the aggrieved party) takes control and effectively starts to run the meeting themselves. If this happens, the practitioner, who will be paying intense attention to what is being said, will allow the meeting to freewheel, ready to draw participants back and take the chair again if it is heading in an unhelpful direction.

Sometimes, people get caught up in the moment, and truths that have been hidden or denied come out unexpectedly. The person responsible is suddenly swept up in honesty. In the middle of her restorative meeting, a woman in prison for causing death by dangerous driving told the mother of the young man who was killed: 'I said before that I didn't see the [red] light because I was too drunk, but I did see it … I used that as an excuse, that I was too drunk to remember.'[14] Having been dealt with by the criminal justice system, there is no further jeopardy if they finally tell the truth, and sometimes they are moved to accept their full responsibility for the first time. For the person they harmed, this truth is like medicine. If the person who made them feel ashamed, soiled and dirty finally 'comes clean', they themselves may feel cleansed. If the version of the offence comes out that matches their memories, but which cannot be verified by anyone else, this can be particularly validating.

Sometimes, the revelation comes from the other side. The individual labelled 'victim' by the criminal justice system is unable to sit quietly through their 'offender's' apology, and talks for the first time about their own culpability: the fact that they were drunk and acting aggressively, they did help spread the rumours, they had slept with so-and-so, left the keys in the car, left the door open. The complexities come out – neat one-sided criminal justice solutions crumble. The two talk it out; what it feels like, what it looks like – they go into it together. In a restorative meeting involving two teenagers and their parents, the young man who had been to court as the 'offender' apologised for assaulting the 'victim' at the fair, although he maintained his story that he only did so in retaliation for a previous assault against his little brother. Perhaps because of the impact of the assault (the 'victim' ended up in hospital, suffering unbearable stomach cramps that were never explained) and his previous record for violence, nobody believed his version of events and the attack was labelled 'unprovoked'. With the apology left hanging in the air and an uneasy silence developing, the 'victim' started to look intensely uncomfortable. Finally, he was unable to contain himself and told the truth, admitting for the first time that he had indeed hit the perpetrator's younger brother. There was an electric silence, everyone was stunned and no one moved. In fact, no one said anything. This confession, that the 'victim's' story had contained lies all along, was left without comment. The perpetrator, who had felt demonised and doubted up to this point, burst into tears. Face to face, what took place at the fair was finally unmasked. Both left looking lighter than when they arrived, with a tangible sense of relief all round, and the mysterious stomach cramps cleared up.

For the restorative meeting really to take off, the parties need to allow the 'other' in through their defences. Normally, we use selective evidence to buttress our own position, the story that we identify with, the 'us' versus 'them'. We feed our inner drama and confirm our long-held convictions that we are the victim and that we are right: that although we are the offender and admit doing it, it wasn't really our fault, and no one has really been affected anyway. The participants may have entered the restorative process to verify their own position, perhaps expecting the worst of the other. If they can suspend their position and let the other in, it takes them out of themselves, and may open the door to empathy. Forgetting their own story, their own drama, they finally truly 'see' the person sitting opposite.

Feelings of being victimised, of 'poor me', reduce or vanish – particularly when we become aware of another person's needs. A man who had been consumed with anger that the couple whose car he stole called the police, which led to him being sent to prison, said "When I saw them sitting there, could see how upset they were, the rage just left." Speaking of his meeting with one of the young men who murdered his son, Ray Donovan said:

> He told us that he'd been a 15-year-old coward. He acknowledged he'd kicked Chris and left him in the road and run away. That was something we'd waited 10 years to hear. He wasn't at all the person we'd expected to see.[15]

Participants may realise that they have mistaken motives, misinterpreted actions, simply missed the fact that when a crime is committed, no one is happy, and everyone suffers. Suddenly, it all comes out, and through shared information, each can pull the other further up the empathy scale. New information provides new awareness and insight into the other, which encourages further sharing and further softening of positions, allowing people to move and shift some more. Sari Stacey speaks movingly of her restorative meeting with the person who burgled her house.[16] He was reluctant to meet her, and soon after sitting down, he gave a mumbled apology, head bowed, unable to make eye contact. When Sari started to talk about the suffering he had caused her and her family, he started to look up at her for the first time. Sari said: 'The moment for me was extremely emotional and, I think for him too. I asked if he had ever thought about the people he had burgled, and he replied that he had never thought about those people, because he "would not have entered the house if they had been there". His perception was that if no one was there it did not matter so much.' Sari then asked: 'Well what were you thinking when you burgled my house?' and he responded: "I didn't think…" When he then went on to say that he was so sorry for what he had done, that he hadn't realised the impact that his burglaries could have, he was a different person.' Suddenly, he was seeing a person sitting there, and she was able to connect with his humanity.

This mutually reinforcing movement I call 'resonant empathy'. It is resonant in the sense that each is responding to and reflecting the other, almost in spite of themselves (see Figure 10.3). As humans, we don't like seeing others suffer, and many people experience an unexpected wave of empathy in the heart of a restorative meeting. 'I just want them to get the help they need' is a sentiment commonly expressed by either party. For Peter Woolf:

> No one, ever, in my whole life, had cared about me like that. Sure, people had looked after me, but only so that I could be more useful to them, that I could fit in with them, do what they wanted. No one had ever expressed concern for me and my feelings, and a desire for me to be a better person. Will and the doctor cared about me and they had no reason to; if anything, the contrary should have been true: they shouldn't have cared about me at all. And because of that, it counted. It mattered. I badly wanted Will and the doctor to be proud of me. I now had a purpose in life. Someone had shown an interest in me, and more than anything in the world I was determined not to let them down.[17]

Each of us has our melting point – the point where we can't maintain our fixed, frozen position in the light of incoming information, where we stop trying to persuade the other to accept our perspective, and allow ourselves to acknowledge their wounds. Dropping those well-

Figure 10.3: Resonant empathy

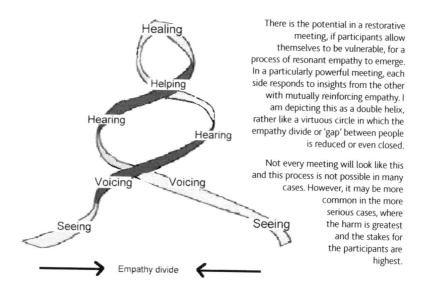

There is the potential in a restorative meeting, if participants allow themselves to be vulnerable, for a process of resonant empathy to emerge. In a particularly powerful meeting, each side responds to insights from the other with mutually reinforcing empathy. I am depicting this as a double helix, rather like a virtuous circle in which the empathy divide or 'gap' between people is reduced or even closed.

Not every meeting will look like this and this process is not possible in many cases. However, it may be more common in the more serious cases, where the harm is greatest and the stakes for the participants are highest.

Seeing – The empathy response may start even as a person enters the room and sees that the other is uncomfortable

Voicing – People often need to feel they have been heard with respect before they can begin to empathise

Hearing – Hearing stories leads to new information and insight, which can lead to further empathy

Helping – Recognising suffering in the other can lead to a spontaneous desire to help

Healing – Healing often happens in the gaps between what is spoken and in the informal chat afterwards, finally closing the gap

established defences allows us to free our imagination, think the unthinkable. Crossing that threshold will be dependent on a mixture of:

- our level of fixedness;
- the quality of the new information;
- our openness and willingness to let go and hear; and
- how safe we feel in the situation.

It can be frustrating if one or both sides remain unable or unwilling to shift, when they don't reach their melting point even in the face of powerful new information and insight from the other. The practitioner may be sitting there hoping, willing, for movement, which doesn't come. In these situations, there is little that the practitioner can do.

The role of others

To explore the dynamics of restorative justice, we have, so far, simplified the process to just two people, who start off as 'victim' and 'offender'. However, for many restorative meetings, it is appropriate to involve a larger circle of people, who may be there because of their involvement in the crime, because they have also been harmed, as bystanders or witnesses to what happened, as supporters for one or both of the parties, or, in some models of restorative practice, as representatives of the community. With a wider audience, those harmed finally get full recognition and acknowledgement of their pain. The person responsible hears it, the practitioner hears it, the supporters hear it, the wider community in the form of community representatives hear it, too; it is not allowed to fade. This often increases empathy in the room, and can be a transformative element in the process. Parents, friends, spouses, siblings, children, neighbours, a police officer, ambulance driver, teacher – all have their own stories to share, indicating just how far the ripples from the crime have travelled. It is likely to have been horrid all round.

Often, it is the perpetrator's parents, siblings or children who are the forgotten victims. Not infrequently, as it emerges that everyone in the room has been affected, everyone has suffered, a shared feeling and common understanding emerges. Seeing the pain, shame and disappointment that they have caused their own loved ones is a powerful way to get through to the person responsible just how much harm they have caused.

The restorative meeting can also give them an opportunity to make the people they love proud of them again, as was the case with an adult prisoner who wanted his children to attend his restorative meeting. In a Referral Order panel involving two girls, one of whom had hit the other over the head with a bottle in a drunken altercation, the parents of both attended the initial panel meeting. The girl who had committed the assault and her parents were reluctant participants,[18] and everyone was feeling raw, aggrieved and suspicious. During the meeting, it quickly emerged how devastating the experience had been all round. The parents saw that they would have acted the same had they been in the other parents' situation, leading to mutual understanding, empathy and respect, and a bond of communality. They observed their daughters revisiting the experience, witnessed an apology from both girls and saw them standing up and shaking hands. Coming away from a meeting that no one had been enthusiastic about, the parents felt relieved, pleased and proud of their daughters. The girls walked off towards the car park together. The practitioner merely held the space for the restorative process to work its magic.

As people in the wider circle talk about how the harmful actions of those responsible have affected them, their role can be pivotal. They ensure that there is adequate disapproval of the poor choices that led to the offence while encouraging everyone who was involved to take responsibility. In a restorative meeting for a case involving a vicious assault, the perpetrator's mother condemned her daughter's actions, but also challenged the 'victim' for her part in the humiliating cyberspace comments, rumours and threats that led up to the incident.

As the meeting progresses, the wider circle becomes a community of care, wishing to look after and keep safe those who have been harmed and sharing a desire for those who caused harm to learn from the experience and change, frequently offering their ideas, commitment and support for ways forward. As the gap with the community closes, as community cohesion increases, both the harmed and the harmer are welcomed in or welcomed back to their community. Absent others can be acknowledged in the room and messages can be recorded to reach out to them. Some meetings have an empty chair for the missing participant.

Judging who gets to come to a restorative meeting is part of the practitioner's art. In some circumstances, small is beautiful, and filling the circle with too many people can water down the restorative process,

Cartoon 10.3: A crowd in between

making it difficult for those involved to share uncomfortable thoughts and feelings. Peter Woolf speaks about how the criminal justice system has a habit of placing more and more people – police, solicitors, magistrates, victim liaison officers, Victim Support volunteers, probation officers, prison staff – between the people most involved in the offence, making communication between them nigh on impossible.[19]

The ripples from a crime spread out far and wide, and there has to be a limit to the number of people invited. Some restorative justice schemes go for large, more formal, 'restorative conferences', others for informal 'victim–offender mediation'. Whichever model is chosen, the practitioner must be confident that adding more people won't be a negative influence on proceedings, and they will spend time meeting everyone in advance, assessing their motives, ensuring that their contribution will be helpful and preparing them for their role. The restorative process is expected to be uncomfortable for the person responsible, but the practitioner must look out for subtle denigration (which may come from their own supporters), and ensure that this part of the conversation focuses on how the supporters and community have been affected rather than allowing them free rein to air their opinions and positions.

Transition

Everyone has now spoken. Different perspectives have been shared about what happened. What now follows is an exploration of the hurtful consequences of the crime, recognising the repercussions for all those whose lives have been touched. To establish the breadth of the impact of the offence, the practitioner may ask participants: 'Who else has been affected?' and 'How have they been affected?' To establish the depth, they may ask: 'What has been the hardest part of this for you?' Crime really does hurt, and even relatively minor offences can have devastating effects.

At this transition stage, when the full consequences of their actions fill the room, the person responsible is invited to speak again. When asked the simple, open question 'Is there anything you would like to say at this point?', an apology is often expressed: 'I am so sorry'; 'Never a day goes by where I don't regret it'; 'I'm so full of remorse.'

It is not uncommon for all communication up to this point to be through the practitioner: the practitioner asking questions and the participants responding back to them. At the transition stage, the parties often start to make eye contact and speak directly with one another for the first time. Sometimes, a striking symmetry of body language and expression starts to emerge: 'I was gutted by what I did. I feel like an idiot'; 'I was gutted to have to call the police, I felt like an idiot.'

If an apology is expressed, unlike the unripe apologies mentioned earlier, this will be a fully informed apology. Reflecting afterwards on the heartfelt apology that was expressed at this point during a restorative meeting, its recipient said: "He was able to be *properly* sorry."

Exploring needs

The stories are fully voiced, the ripples of harm have been exposed, it's time to shift the focus from the past to the future. From how bad things have been to how much better they can become. A question the practitioner may ask at this point is, 'What do you need to feel better?'

Once again, it is usually best to start with the person who caused harm. If the person harmed is asked first to come up with ideas about what would help them, the person responsible will often simply agree to everything they are asking, without giving the question much thought. This can let them off the hook: having responded to the other person's ideas, they are less likely to come forward with their own. If asked first, it is such an open question that they may say something about themselves – 'I need to get help with my anger', 'I need to stop hanging round with those people' – or about those they harmed – 'I will feel better if you accept my apology', 'I need you to know that I

Cartoon 10.4: The same as mine

have changed and I won't hurt you again'. 'What do you need to feel better?' is not a question likely to be asked of defendants in court – but it can be a useful and disarming opening as the meeting starts to explore participants' needs. The person responsible may make a link to the unmet needs and perhaps the unhappiness that led to the offence.

Unless these are all expressed spontaneously, the practitioner may refer people back to the needs identified during the restorative enquiries; in our example in Chapter Six, the needs were for recognition, support, appreciation, safety, reassurance and respect. These underlying needs are fundamental human needs. If one side or the other says 'I need to feel safe', 'I need my experience to be recognised', 'I need to feel respected', 'I need support or cooperation', those are needs that we can all sign up to.

Notes

[1] There is a chapter on co-facilitation in Wallis, P. and Fast, E. (2013) *Restorative justice facilitator training trainee manual*, London: Youth Justice Board, p 58.

[2] Nodding, J. (2011) Jo's Story, Resolution #40, Spring 2011, Restorative Justice Council, London p7 (see also Video Resources, Appendix).

[3] 'Behind the Hoodie' (https://vimeo.com/23797353).

[4] http://theforgivenessproject.com

[5] Goode, M. and Goode, J. (2001) 'An experience of restorative justice', unpublished.

[6] 'The conversation', *The Guardian*, 21 May 2011.

[7] Pranis, K. (2002) 'Restorative values and confronting family violence', in H. Strang and J. Braithwaite (eds) *Restorative justice and family violence*, Cambridge: Cambridge University Press, p 31.

[8] 'The conversation', *The Guardian*, 21 May 2011.

[9] Woolf, P. (2008) *The damage done*, London: Bantam Books, see p 87.

[10] www.telegraph.co.uk/news/uknews/law-and-order/8377905/Who-would-honestly-want-to-go-and-meet-the-man-who-raped-you.html

[11] 'The conversation', *The Guardian*, 21 May 2011.

[12.] Woolf, P. (2008) *The damage done*, London: Bantam Books, p 306.

[13.] Claire's story can be found at www.telegraph.co.uk/news/uknews/crime/8378549/Dr-Claire-Chung-has-a-right-to-be-angry.html and at www.telegraph.co.uk/news/uknews/crime/9716234/Why-I-must-speak-out-to-stop-my-rapist-being-freed.html

[14.] Miller, S. (2011) *After the crime*, New York, NY: New York University Press, p 116.

[15.] http://tinyurl.com/og56npf

[16.] Sari's story can be found in Lummer, R., Nahrwold, M. and Süß, B. (eds) (2012) *Restorative justice – a victim perspective and issues of co-operation*, Keil: Fachhochschule, p 129. Thames Valley Restorative Justice Service now has a European-funded, 'victim-led' project specifically geared for people harmed by crime to access restorative justice.

[17.] Woolf, P. (2008) *The damage done*, London: Bantam Books, p 309.

[18.] In Referral Order panel meetings, unlike other restorative meetings, the person harmed has the right to be invited into this criminal justice process, which means the perpetrator has limited choice.

[19.] Woolf, P. (2008) *The damage done*, London: Bantam Books.

Part Five
Empathy Level Four: helping

'I'd like to be able to say sorry properly to you and your family. I don't know how, though?! So if you ever need any help with anything, I'd be there without hesitation. Gardening, decorating … anything. Honestly, please just ask me.'

(Tylah)[1]

CHAPTER ELEVEN

'Doing sorry'

Finally, the focus shifts to future plans, introduced by the practitioner with the question: 'How can we take this forward?' Considering how everyone's needs will best be met, restorative meetings often arrive at creative, healing solutions, which are more likely to be successful because they are suggested, and are being owned by, the people most directly connected with the offence.

The restorative process now opens up the opportunity for repair. The first meaning of responsibility explored in Chapter Seven is accepting culpability: 'Yes, I admit that I did my part in it, I was responsible.' The second meaning is being accountable: 'I am responsible for putting this right.' This responsibility or 'ability to respond' can be expressed through reparation, and it isn't uncommon for spontaneous offers of reparation to be made at this stage in the restorative meeting.

Moving forward

We can't wipe out what we have done in the past – although people who commit crimes often express a wish that they could. Overcoming feelings of guilt and taking responsibility for our actions can be a complex process. A few words of spoken apology may not be able to undo this knot. As one young man said to the person he had offended against: "Sorry isn't good enough." The entanglements created by crime may be too great, may require more than a word or a phrase – no matter how heartfelt – to release them.

A very concrete step that can be transformative for both sides is reparation. Offers of reparation have melting, gap-closing power, and during the meeting, the practitioner occasionally has to step in to stop the person responsible enthusiastically offering unrealistic sums of money – or all their waking hours – to make amends. Genuine reparation doesn't focus on the self, but on the needs of the other. Reparation can be symbolic or material: a letter, a gift or financial compensation for loss. Practical reparation in the form of a task is particularly helpful, in making concrete that expressed desire to help. A task is tangible, and the person harmed can 'see' the extent to which their offender is sorry by the effort they are willing to put in. One person harmed called it 'doing sorry'; that is, one step beyond 'being' sorry. Reparation is physical proof of remorse.

While reparation aims to benefit those harmed, the process is equally helpful for the person taking responsibility: it helps to help. A practical reparation task can disentangle those feelings of guilt, shame and remorse.

It's not uncommon for people to work at reparation like demons when they feel that it is directly undoing the harm they caused: failing to take breaks, wanting to continue when the task is complete, experiencing (for the first time in some cases) the joy of giving. In a real sense, they are atoning for the harm they caused. Using their time, sweat, skill and creativity they work at effacing their guilt, which may reduce or even transform their underlying shame.

Reparation can contain a little of the restorative magic. When a young man driving a stolen car crashed, destroying a couple's wall, watching him carefully rebuild it was somehow symbolic of rebuilding a relationship, closing the gap brick by brick. An old man whose fence had been damaged kept glancing out of his window at the youth repairing it, sceptical, a little wary initially and then gradually softening, coming out to chat and finally to help. Good reparation lifts both parties up the scale of empathy, until each starts to see the other's humanity. When a student was told that the person who stole his bike was willing to build him a new one, he suggested that they do it together: what could be more healing than the two of them chatting over that task?

Some people don't want the person responsible to do anything for them. They may prefer them to do some voluntary work for others or make a donation to a good cause. They may start the meeting thinking that they will want reparation, and by the end realise that what they really want is emotional resolution, or simply for the person who harmed them to make a real effort to keep out of trouble.

Negotiating outcomes

As reparation is discussed and reassurances offered, some restorative meetings move to an outcome agreement or contract, negotiated and signed by all. It may simply be an affirmation of the main sense of the meeting – the sentiments, promises and assurances made. It may be more specific, in which case, the practitioner will ensure that it is SMART,[2] clarify who is committing to what and establish monitoring arrangements. For people who are likely to meet again outside of a controlled meeting, the agreement often contains quite detailed undertakings of what will happen in a chance encounter: 'If I see you in the street, I will cross over and carry on walking without looking at you'; or 'It is okay to say "Hi", but I don't want to be your friend.' One young man told me that once he was released from prison, he framed his outcome agreement and hung it on the wall of his bedroom as a reminder of the reassurances he had made to the person he had harmed, which included his personal commitment to keep out of trouble in future. In domestic violence cases (including those involving sibling aggression and adolescent-on-parent violence), the outcome agreement may outline safe boundaries for the relationship.

Ideally, the search for ways forward will become a joint project, both parties pitching in their ideas. Offers of help can go both ways, and the agreement may be less about what one can do for the other, and more about finding the best way forward for all. As far as possible, the practitioner will avoid offering their own opinions or solutions, particularly when they haven't been invited. Their task is to keep an eye on the agreement reached to check that it is realistic and proportionate to the offence.

Here, the wider circle may come into its own. Aunts, uncles and grandparents are particularly good at offering help and ensuring compliance. One of the delights of restorative justice is the unexpected nature of some of the suggestions. A slightly awkward meeting between two young men who had fought one another during a youth club session was transformed when the youth worker present said that what would help him to feel better would be to see them shaking hands (They did!). A woman who heard that the young man who had burgled her was a talented artist asked whether he would be willing to create a picture for her. She was delighted by the result.

There may be an agreement about further meetings, particularly if the parties were previously known and are likely to meet one another again, or are living in the same house. In these cases, a chance to review and monitor progress will be important. They may have used the restorative meeting to renegotiate their relationship, so that they can coexist safely, and may like to review how this is going.

It is vital that promises be kept. Any slippage will lead to a slide back down the empathy scale for one or both parties. If the person responsible reneges on a commitment, it reinforces any lingering suspicion that they don't care after all. In one case, a woman who was approached by a restorative practitioner declined involvement in any restorative process. Her reason was that she had felt aggrieved at not receiving a promised apology letter from a totally unrelated incident four years previously. She hadn't forgotten. Contracts and outcome agreements must indicate how compliance by the person responsible will be monitored, which may be a role for the perpetrator's case manager or, more informally, for their family or community.

Endings

Many people harmed by crime – even in the most serious cases – want nothing for themselves, but ask for a commitment from the person responsible that they will seek help and, above all, not do it again, not to them, not to anyone. They know first-hand how devastating it has been and want reassurance that lessons have been learned, and that no one else will have to suffer what they have been through. If it is the person harmed who sets this task, it can be a strong motivator for the person responsible. Peter Woolf recalls the moment when the practitioner asked the people he had burgled, 'What would you like to happen to Peter?':

> I thought they were going to say 'Give him 100 lashings.'
> But to my amazement, they said they would like to see me
> do well – beat my addiction and get some qualifications. It
> was mind boggling. It was like being shown respect for the
> first time as a human being. It's changed my life.[3]

A final question that may be asked of everyone by the practitioner is: 'What do you hope will come out of this meeting?' This is a beautifully open question. Sometimes, the answer focuses on the self: 'I hope that I learn my lesson.' Most often, though, the answer contains a wish or a hope for the other person: 'I hope that you feel better'; 'I hope you get the help you need'; 'I hope that you can now put this behind you.' The journey from thinking about self to thinking about other is complete.

Many restorative meetings end with tea, coffee and refreshments. The practitioner may find an excuse to busy themselves in a corner of the room – perhaps to make copies of the outcome agreement – as this can be a time when people relax, chat, talk about friends, family and community, talk about other things, make or rebuild connections, agree to draw a line, and pull closed what remains of the gap. For Ray and Vi Donovan:

> The most important part of the process is the tea and biscuits
> after the official meeting. With the second boy [who had
> been involved in their son's killing], after the meeting we
> talked for four hours. He's a plasterer learning the trade, and
> he told us all about his girlfriend and the baby that's on the

way. Neither of us had to stay for the tea and biscuits – but it was the most healing part.[4]

After the meeting, the practitioner has much work still to do. They will reflect on the process and their own practice, ideally discussing the meeting with their co-facilitator and line manager while it is fresh. They will seek feedback from everyone who attended. Sometimes, after a particularly emotional meeting, the perpetrator's mood can dip, even if they are saying the opposite. The practitioner will ensure that there is support and arrange for someone, perhaps a personal officer if they are in prison, to keep an eye on them in the hours and days that follow. There may also be recording, monitoring of outcome agreements, evaluation and review meetings to organise.

The practitioner's role

Looking back over the practitioner's role overall, their prime function is to ensure that it is easy for people to opt for a restorative process if they wish to, and to keep the process as safe as possible. Reflecting on the restorative justice practitioner training that he had just finished, and the skills practice using the restorative language described throughout this book, one training participant said that it felt a bit prescribed. But there is a clear logic to the process and keeping close to the themes and restorative questions allows the practitioner to feel (almost) total confidence when bringing people together to talk about serious conflict, strong emotions, deep hurt. Once those skills are mastered and internalised, the practitioner can use them with freedom. Taking the process for a restorative meeting from start to finish, the practitioner has a range of roles (see Box 11.1).

Despite all of the skilful means at their disposal, the parts of the meeting when the practitioner says little or nothing are the most powerful, when the participants own the process and simply converse and connect with one another in their own way. In most meetings, there are few major surprises for the practitioner; following weeks, months or even possibly years of preparation (for the most serious cases), they largely know what people are likely to say, although the meetings always feel fresh, with new pieces of information or aspects of the stories that haven't been mentioned before.

Participants in a restorative process are often unaware of the significant skills and experience that the practitioner brings to the role. When Mark Umbreit and colleagues worked with people who had suffered extreme violence in Texas and Ohio, their clients expressed a wish to:

Box 11.1: The practitioner's role

• **To listen:** hearing everyone's perspective.
• **To offer:** building on people's desire to engage in a restorative process, offering to facilitate that process for them.
• **To arrange:** making all the logistical arrangements for the meeting.
• **To facilitate:** placing some boundaries round the process to keep it safe.
• **To enable:** ensuring that everyone can speak and listen.
• **To allow:** letting go of control so that the dynamic of the restorative process can take over.
• **To vanish:** disappearing completely if things are going well, shifting back their chair, looking down at their feet.
• **To clarify:** picking up some control again to ensure that outcome agreements are SMART.
• **To monitor and support:** carefully following up on the meeting so that benefits aren't lost.
• **To record, reflect, evaluate** and so on.

> be in the hands of highly competent mediators who take time to know them, who listen profoundly, who validate their feelings and experience, who help them identify what they want to accomplish, and who then step out of the way during the actual dialogue, so that participants themselves can own the process.[5]

It can look deceptively simple from the outside. Is it rocket science? No, but in its own way, taking on the role of restorative practitioner can sometimes feel as challenging.

Notes

[1] Tylah burgled Linda Lowne's house in September 2011, while she and her husband and five children were asleep upstairs. See Restorative Justice Council (2013) 'Linda's story', *Resolution*, Autumn, p 10.

[2] An acronym used by people in the field, standing for Specific, Measurable, Achievable, Realistic and Time-limited.

[3] Home Office magazine *The Sharp End*, p 8 (date unknown).

[4] http://tinyurl.com/og56npf

[5] Umbreit, M.S., Vos, B., Coates, R.B. and Brown, K.A. (2003) *Facing violence: The path of restorative justice and dialogue*, New York, NY: Criminal Justice Press, p 335.

CHAPTER TWELVE

Does it always go so well?

The most common question asked of the restorative practitioner is: 'Does it ever go wrong?' The glib answer is: 'No – it doesn't go wrong – unless the practitioner is at fault.' The process of assessment should identify when a person who caused harm is asking for communication with those they harmed for the wrong reason: to threaten, manipulate or intimidate them. It should identify if communication is simply unwise, for example, reinforcing contact between someone convicted of a stalking offence and the person they are stalking. It should identify if the person harmed is unable to advocate for themselves: if they are too raw, fragile or enraged to benefit (although, in practice, those people usually deselect themselves).

Careful preparation and timing ensure that people are willing and ready and know roughly what to expect, the practitioner checking with each person: 'How would you feel/what would you say if X said such-and-such?' Expert facilitation keeps the process as safe as possible, with particularly careful planning (eg time out, use of a co-facilitator, extra supporters, breakout spaces) for complex and sensitive cases. Using the maxim 'We look for repair, and in doing so, we cause no further harm', the restorative practitioner simply doesn't risk bringing people together in one room if, somewhere in their gut, they feel that it could go either way. Down (the empathy scale) is not an option.

Some services rule out certain categories of crime, asserting that it isn't safe to bring people together in cases involving, for example, rape, murder, hate crime or domestic violence. There may certainly be stronger dynamics of manipulation, control and denial coming from the person responsible in such cases, demanding particular care in establishing their motives, although the literature contains plenty of examples of successful meetings. An argument against excluding offence categories from a restorative service is that, in most of these cases, the people were previously known to one another, and are likely to meet one another again anyway – sooner or later. How much better for that first encounter to be at a carefully managed meeting rather than a random bumping into one another on a street corner. And as Claire Chung said to me, reflecting on her meeting with the man who raped her: "If not an offer of restorative justice, what else? Victims may currently feel they have nothing else."

Difficult cases where the ice won't melt

Difficult cases for the practitioner to handle include those involving disputed harm, differing stories, murky memories and slippery facts. Fixed positions where one or both parties start particularly low down the empathy scale constitute the most dangerous ground, where the gap is biggest, and risk assessment most crucial; where a restorative meeting is likely to be neutral at best, and things could potentially get worse, without expert handling. If people aren't letting down their defences, the meeting is riskier, and explicit ground rules leading to a more structured and tightly controlled meeting will be required. In these cases, most or all communication will be addressed in a triangle, to and from the practitioner rather than directly between the parties, until and unless things shift, and people feel able to make eye contact with one another. There is quite a skill in judging when to allow difficult emotions to be vented, and when to pull on the reins if an exchange is proving unproductive. *In extremis*, the practitioner is prepared to call a break or even to stop the meeting to halt a situation where one or both parties are sliding down the empathy scale.

While everyone's need to tell the story in their own way is okay, as mentioned in Chapter Eleven, it is important to avoid a tit-for-tat argument about specific 'facts', which will almost invariably be fruitless and potentially harmful. Resonant empathy creates a virtuous spiral – which I think of as a double helix of mutually reinforcing empathy between the antagonists (see Figure 10.3). If a meeting descends into a tit-for-tat argument, there is a danger of the exact opposite: a vicious circle of accusation and defiance. To avoid disputes over facts, the restorative process instead places emphasis on what people were thinking and feeling as events unfolded, rather than conducting another investigation to establish the 'truth'. Thoughts and feelings cannot be disputed and are safer ground to explore than details of an incident that happened some time ago and that everyone will have experienced and remembered differently. If a difficult encounter is anticipated, it can help to encourage everyone at the start to be honest and gentle with one another and to accept that people's perspectives will differ.

While a poor meeting may simply confirm and reinforce positions, maintaining the empathy divide, a disastrous meeting can lead to someone being hurt, storming out of the room (sometimes halfway through the meeting) feeling worse than when they arrived. If both just want to be there to cement a position, both risk dragging each other down the empathy scale. Unless at least one party is open to hear, nothing will be heard, and the gap becomes wider than ever – even if people are sitting in the same room. The practitioner must accept that some gaps can't be bridged, and a restorative encounter shouldn't always be attempted.

Unfortunately, it isn't always clear from the outset whether positions will remain frozen. We've seen that people arriving in the room are likely to be anxious, and carry with them preconceived ideas about the other person. They may be unable to listen to what the other has to say until they themselves have been heard, and a meeting can turn quite suddenly – can become positive and even transformative from an unpromising start.

Ultimately, participants will only be involved in restorative justice to the degree they choose, will get as much out of the process as they put into it. Having made the offer of a restorative process, the practitioner accepts and honours the responses they receive, supports participants no matter where they are at, no matter where they want to go next in their journey. The practitioner is not there to place judgement on people if they aren't able to melt, can't let go, don't wish to seek or offer repair, aren't ready to move on.

The practitioner can't manipulate the gap to close, and stories of practitioners who try to force the issue fill one with dread. Marian Liebmann shares a story of a poor Referral Order panel meeting involving Mark, a young man who has mild learning difficulties, and Jack, who assaulted him in school. Jack's grandfather had just died and he had been in tears. He noticed Mark looking at him with curiosity across the playground, and perceiving a smile on his face, Jack went over and hit him. Because of legal time frames, preparation for the panel was poor: there had only been one pre-meeting with Jack and nobody met his mother in advance:

> The panel started off badly. The panel leader was nervous. She missed out some crucial groundrules, and was then unable to curb the frequent interruptions. She asked Jack to explain what happened. He refused, and became emotional and angry when asked about his grandfather's death. His mother constantly interrupted, minimising the offence and trying to shift the blame on to Mark. The Youth Offending Team officer tried to rescue something for the victims by asking Jack directly to apologise to Mark. This was like a red rag to a bull. Jack was clearly an unhappy young man who had shown no remorse at all for the offence. He laid into the victim with verbal abuse and abusive hand gestures. The victim worker quickly led Mark and his mother out.[1]

This is where adequate preparation, and training and guidance for the practitioner, are vital. Sitting across from someone who has harmed you but refuses to speak, clearly has no regrets about their actions, is told to apologise or, worst still, is abusive will be re-victimising. Trying to make things right with someone who just wants to abuse or punish you will make you feel worse and more inclined to do it again. These situations are avoidable, while stories of harmful restorative justice practice set back the cause for everyone.

Don't give up

One of the abiding mysteries of restorative justice is that the practitioner may not be the best judge of success. A meeting can appear to have been a failure, a resolution may feel shallow or seemingly non-existent, but the movement and melting can carry on afterwards, even if the two people are not in contact. It may not *look* like a great ending, but this may not be the case (even in the previous example, Mark and his mother said that they were glad that they had attended). It has become much more difficult for people to carry on with their projection of the 'other', which has been changed by the encounter. The practitioner must remember that it is not their story, not their process, to not get hooked on outcomes. Who knows what the impact may be in 10 years' time?

Satisfaction rates following restorative meetings are high, especially for those harmed. Perpetrators often come out feeling relieved and proud. One young man reflected: "He seemed to be more interested in me as a person than as a criminal." The practitioner will be keen to receive everyone's feedback, both in person and through evaluation forms.

In my own experience, restorative meetings almost always go better than anticipated. I deliberately keep participants' expectations low, and then, on the day, everyone (almost) invariably rises to the occasion, sharing more than they expected, moving from their previously held positions. Perhaps it is the mysterious process of 'resonant empathy' at work, the gap-closing movement that can only happen during a restorative meeting.

Despite this, and while participants often express complete satisfaction with the process, for the practitioner, there can still be a lingering feeling that it could have gone better, that while it went as well as it could have in light of where everyone was at the start, somehow it didn't completely repair the harm or fully heal the wounds. Providing it doesn't become disempowering, this dissatisfaction can usefully drive a desire to learn from each meeting, to improve on the next.

Note
[1] Liebmann, M. (2007) *Restorative justice, how it works*, London: Jessica Kingsley Publishers, p 319.

Part Six
Empathy Level Five: healing

When we have victimised or have been victimised, the journey from brokenness and isolation to transcendence and belonging requires us to re-narrate our stories so that they are no longer just about shame and humiliation but ultimately about dignity and triumph.

(Howard Zehr)[1]

CHAPTER THIRTEEN

Into the heart of restorative justice

As we enter the heart of restorative justice, normally well-grounded and sober practitioners are sometimes so moved by its potential that they start using mystical, even religious, language to describe the process. A colleague recently said: "It's truly amazing, magical." Restorative meetings are always interesting but it is not uncommon for those who have attended a particularly powerful restorative meeting to say that it stands out as the high point in their long career as a social worker, police officer, prison chaplain or probation officer. The parties involved can also sound evangelical, wishing to share their stories and encourage others to give restorative justice a try, as a glance at the stories on the Why Me?[2] and Restorative Justice Council websites will show. This chapter considers some of the features of restorative justice, and may explain why it can bring out the mystic in the most sceptical among us.

Shame, guilt and empathy

Drawing on studies from Japanese culture, the Australian criminologist John Braithwaite introduced the influential theory of 'reintegrative shaming', which involves the evocation of shameful feelings in the person responsible during a restorative meeting.[3] He asserted that shame can be utilised in both a good and bad manner. Criminal justice focuses on negative, or 'stigmatic', shaming, with punishment labelling individuals as immoral agents. Braithwaite called this 'disintegrative shaming', which he said is counterproductive because 'offenders' take on these negative labels and react negatively by reoffending, which 'divides the community by creating a class of outcasts'.[4]

Braithwaite argued that 'shaming' can have a positive impact if it is used in the right way, and that the restorative process is itself a 'positive' form of shaming. If family members and other supporters are invited into a restorative meeting, the restorative process provides additional shaming through their shows of disapproval and regret, because the shame which 'matters most' in Braithwaite's view is the shame arising from the disapproval of the people we care about – not the police or the judges.

Braithwaite stressed that shame should only be evoked in a way that condemns the offending behaviour without degrading or stigmatising the perpetrator. He said that shame can then be constructive because the person responsible is not labelled as bad, and having experienced shame, the focus can turn to how he or she can make amends and be 'reintegrated' as a member of the law-abiding community.

There are several potential pitfalls when shaming becomes an objective in restorative justice. Braithwaite kept a broad definition of 'shaming' to include 'all societal processes of expressing social disapproval which have the intention or effect of invoking remorse in the person being shamed and/or condemnation by others who become aware of the shaming'.[5] Even so, the concept can easily be misinterpreted or distorted. Anyone having a disapproving finger pointed at them to condemn their actions is likely to become defensive and either keep quiet or fight back, and Braithwaite has written many times that the theory advises against this. Although not writing in the context of restorative justice, Brene Brown observes that, 'When we feel shame, we are most likely to protect ourselves by blaming something or someone, rationalising our lapse, offering a disingenuous apology, or hiding out.'[6] Braithwaite's experiments found that when this is their reaction, bullying of the shamed person by other participants increases (although conversely if the reaction of the person responsible is 'shame acknowledgement', bullying is reduced).[7] Participants (or practitioners) may miss the vital distinction between condemning the behaviour rather than the person, and the person responsible, through having their behaviour 'shamed', may come to feel that they are shameful people, even if this is not intended. If shaming the perpetrator in order to reduce reoffending is the practitioner's desired outcome, there is a risk that the process is used to get a 'result' for the criminal justice system (and it may not be the agenda for the person harmed). Finally, many people who commit crime have already experienced negative forms of shaming built up through undermining messages received since earliest childhood, their crimes arising because they feel bad about themselves and who they are. The prison psychologist James Gilligan wrote that shame is 'the primary or ultimate cause of all violence'.[8] Braithwaite saw the restorative process as a way through shame to remorse and reintegration, but there is a danger that a practice that interprets Braithwaite's concept of shaming the behaviour to mean setting out to shame, as in wagging a finger of disapproval, risks adding to the shame that led to the crime in the first place, without addressing those deeper underlying needs.

Braithwaite's reintegrative shaming theory has been tested empirically in Australia in the 're-integrative shaming experiments' (RISE). The research found reduced reoffending for people attending diversionary restorative justice conferences based on reintegrative shaming, compared to those attending a court hearing.[9] Allison Morris has since queried the findings, raising the suggestion that 'another way of interpreting these data is that empathy or understanding the effects of offending on victims was the trigger'.[10]

The focus of restorative justice shared in this book is based upon storytelling and its potential to elicit empathy rather than shaming, although, ultimately the difference may be in emphasis and semantics; the points made here about the differing effects of shame and guilt are the same as Braithwaite's distinction between stigmatization and reintegrative shaming, and in a restorative meeting the interplay of shame, guilt, empathy and reintegration are all interconnected. In all restorative justice models, everyone is invited to share their experience of the crime and to listen to the stories of others. Because these narratives are about the participants and arise from their own experience of the offence (which is likely to have been a negative experience for everyone), they tend to open up a creative and empathetic space. Sometimes, harmful actions are condemned, although as the stories are told, the focus may move away from a simple bad choice made by the person responsible on the day of the crime to the deeper unmet needs that led to the offending behaviour. Shameful feelings may also arise, and can be seen through someone's body language and the heat rising in their face. For Peter Woolf, 'the shame of what I'd done ran up and down inside me … I felt hot and then cold and couldn't look at anyone.'[11] However, this is a natural response, and in an empathetic environment, it is more likely to be a rising of conscience making people feel guilty, rather than shaming coming from outside. Harris et al write that 'shame … occurs when one feels disapproval in the eyes of others (imagined or real disapproval); guilt occurs when one disapproves of one's own behaviour (disapproval by one's own conscience)'.[12] Braithwaite acknowledges that this 'indirect' form of shaming (in which the wrongdoer is the one who condemns their own actions) is likely to be the most reintegrative.

Shame is a complex notion, with elements of social rejection and feelings of personal failure. Brown distinguishes between shame ('You are bad') and guilt ('You did something bad'). She asserts that shame, which she describes as 'the intensely painful feeling or experience of believing that we are flawed and therefore unworthy of love or belonging', is negative. Guilt, however, she calls 'very adaptive'.[13] To accept guilt is hard and uncomfortable. We have to allow that what we have done has affected others, may have caused them hurt and anguish. Brown could be talking about a restorative meeting when she describes the importance of accepting when we have made a mistake, exposing our vulnerability, showing our imperfect selves to others. To feel better, the person responsible will have to reach out to connect to the very people he or she has harmed, not knowing which way it might go.

Guilt is an unpleasant feeling and one that is hard to shift. It is also a necessary emotion. Guilt is nature's way of making us look back over our actions, reconsider our motives, take responsibility for our behaviour. Accepting guilt and doing something about it takes courage, and, as a result, it may also release the individual not only from their guilt over specific actions, but also from some of their underlying shame. This is partly because in allowing them to see beyond their own to the other person's pain, they are taken out of their shameful selves. Brown says that 'The antidote for shame is empathy... if we can share our story with someone who responds with empathy and understanding, shame can't survive.'[14] By rebuilding relationships with others, it allows them to find their way back to connection.

Doing something about guilt can give the person responsible the experience of pride and self-worth. Crime is doing the wrong thing, making amends is doing the right thing, and in doing the right thing, there is action and energy. Kelvin, who committed a string of burglaries under the influence of drugs, writes:

> I had a lot of friends who supported me [in deciding to go to a restorative meeting]. They were ringing me up the moment I came out, saying 'Well done, Kelv!' It really put me on top of the world and made me think; if I can do this, what can't I do?[15]

The facilitator may see the relief on the face of the person responsible, some of whom express amazement that the person they harmed treated them with respect – despite their own feelings of unworthiness.

Shame is also a common reaction for those harmed by crime. A restorative process can carry a powerful message for people who may have taken on responsibility for what happened: that they were not to blame, that they couldn't have done anything to stop it happening. As one participant in a restorative meeting said: "I could stop hating myself and put the responsibility back where it should be."

Melissa was molested by her father between the ages of 10 and 15. When he finally turned himself in and admitted the abuse to the police, Melissa's relief at finally being safe was overshadowed by guilt about his arrest and imprisonment and shame over the 'family secret'. Facing him in a restorative meeting gave her back her power. Crucially, her father repeated that the abuse hadn't been her fault. She comments on the experience:

> I am no longer sitting there ripping myself apart that I let this happen. He did this, not me. There is no longer the constant haunting nightmares and invasion into my daily thoughts. I am not as fearful. I feel greater comfort in talking about what happened. [The restorative process] took the burden and guilt off me. I don't feel shameful anymore.[16]

Responsibility and accountability

> Until you are honest with yourself and face your past, the past continues. Until you admit guilt and take responsibility for your offense, the offense continues. Until you become accountable beyond yourself to your victim and your community, there can be no healing. (David Doerfler[17])

A common principle that is shared by both criminal justice and restorative justice is to hold people who commit crimes to account for their actions. In both processes, responsibility for the perpetrator is defined, agreed and then reinforced.

So far in this book, I have introduced two meanings for the word 'responsibility'. The first looks to the past, and is about culpability ('I accept what I did'); the second is in the present, and is about obligation ('I need to sort this out'). There is a third meaning, which looks to the future, and is about accountability ('It won't happen again'). Restorative justice only works when people are starting to engage with the first meaning of responsibility, and this is where the criminal justice system is essential. At the point of lowest empathy, when people are trying to wriggle out of their responsibility for causing harm, the police identify and apprehend the 'offender', the courts separate out the innocent from the guilty, and the law provides a framework of compulsion that takes away the freedom of those responsible, without which the restorative justice practitioner would struggle to have that initial conversation about what happened. Once the person responsible is engaging in a restorative process, the information and insights received directly from the people harmed by their offence can be a powerful way to clarify exactly what they are culpable of, and to challenge any tendency they may have to neutralise their responsibility for what happened.

The criminal justice system is beginning to recognise that, having caught the perpetrator in its web, the second aspect of responsibility is best met through a restorative process. Instead of being a passive receiver of punishment, perpetrators are actively challenged to consider what they have done and what they need to do now to sort things out. This is likely to be uncomfortable and even painful. The criminal justice system's attempts to force people to pay back to those they harm, for example, through a Compensation Order, are a blunt tool that can fail to address the deeper needs of those involved, and that can sometimes make things worse. The opposite of injustice is not justice but healing, and, as we have seen, healing comes through empathy rather than simply 'just deserts'.

The third aspect of responsibility is one where criminal justice and restorative justice can work well together, through a system described here as 'parallel justice'. Rehabilitation is a stated aim of the criminal justice system, but one that some feel it struggles with.[18] For more serious and persistent offenders, and particularly those who end up in prison, recidivism figures remain stubbornly high. Traditionally, criminal justice resources follow outcomes (and we are entering a world of payment by result), while for those resources to be most effective, they should follow needs. Restorative conversations help people to identify the deeper needs leading up to and arising from the offence, which can help criminal justice agencies to set up systems to meet those needs, rather than putting the system first. This could also help to restore the balance of resources away from its overwhelming emphasis on the perpetrator's needs at the expense of those harmed.

Those harmed by crime typically start their journey blaming themselves. Even those who were in no way responsible take too much responsibility for acts that were simply not their fault. This may be an attempt to make sense out of a senseless situation, to find some control where control has been taken away. At least if they blame themselves, they can do something about it.

The restorative process restores their power, puts them back in control, takes them out of the role of 'victim' or 'survivor'. One man who attended a restorative meeting expressed this graphically: "It was like the balance of justice had tipped, and it was back in my favour." In choosing the difficult path of restorative justice, those harmed are actively taking responsibility for their own well-being and recovery.

Although they were not responsible for what happened and mustn't be made to feel responsible for stopping it happening again, some people do choose to assume some responsibility for what happens next for the perpetrator. Claire Chung, having met the man who had raped her, decided that she didn't trust the criminal justice system to deliver on safety. Knowing that the offence had occurred within hours of her attacker being released from prison, she used her restorative meeting to share those feelings with the probation service. Like many people involved in restorative justice, she wanted regular feedback on his engagement with his sentence.

In 'The conversation', Kathleen also assumed responsibility for the man who burgled her house while recognising that, ultimately, she had to let go and allow him to turn his life around:

> Kathleen: "I was hoping that you would change, which you have, and it's good to hear that you're doing so well. You've got to think about your freedom, you don't want to be locked up again. I've tried to get you back on track. But now it's up to you. Just keep up the good work."

> Reggie: "I will. Whenever I'm feeling down or in that mould of where I used to be, I always, always think of you and it keeps me going forward."

> Kathleen: "Never look back, always look forward."[19]

It shouldn't be necessary for the person harmed to carry the burden of responsibility for keeping the person who harmed them on track, although others who are present in the meeting – in particular, those holding responsibility for supervising or monitoring the perpetrator – may assume this role. Essentially, though, the restorative process is designed to bring closure so that everyone can move on with their lives. For the person responsible, this may be a long journey in which they have to face up to those they hurt, to their community and, most importantly, to themselves.

Looking back at the figures in Box 1.1, it is difficult to avoid the conclusion that many 'offenders' (at least those in custody for more persistent and/or serious offending) have been failed by society. The individuals in that list were forced to cope in abusive homes, unsafe neighbourhoods and, in some cases, barren or even harmful institutions.

These are not excuses, but they go some way to explaining how they could do what they did. Without condoning their actions, the people they have harmed often gain insight during a restorative meeting into the damage and loss that their tormentors have suffered, can start to trace back, in the story they hear, the pressures towards the crime they suffered. In wanting to prevent them ever doing it again, those harmed may feel accountable not only to the person who offended against them, but also to people who commit crime in general. Since society failed to provide these people with safe, nurturing childhoods, demanding punishment and exacting revenge will not provide the resolution they crave.

It is not uncommon for people who have been through a restorative process (including the wider circle of family, supporters and community representatives) to offer their services to volunteer in criminal justice. In showing concern for the person who caused harm and others on the same destructive path, they are not suddenly becoming do-gooders. They understand that as we are all connected, we are all 'responsible' in the widest sense for the wrongs in society, because bad things don't happen in isolation. They are taking the restoration of this interconnection to its logical conclusion, by seeking to break the cycle of crime.

Stuckness and movement

People who experience a serious crime can become stuck, unable to move on. For them, the experience remains as vivid as if it was yesterday. Two sisters of a man who was murdered during a robbery went through periods when they would speak to one another on the phone every day for an hour about their brother – 15 years after his death.[20] When this happens, those around them become frustrated that they don't seem able to 'move on' and find 'closure', and as the concern and sympathy dries up, they can feel increasingly isolated. Sometimes, the only way to move forward, to get out of stuckness, is to embark on a restorative journey.

The melting power of restorative justice is the process where new and unexpected insight makes it hard for people to stay fixed in their positions, unable to maintain their prejudices in spite of themselves. With these awakening moments, their carefully constructed images of the 'other', usually based upon poor information, melt away.

Movement can come suddenly, and it is amazing how quickly people can lose a long-held animosity. When one or both parties make a seismic shift, there is undoubtedly magic in the room. For the practitioner who has supported the parties to this point – perhaps even more than those engrossed in the process (who may not realise at the time what is happening) – it is the distance travelled in a meeting that is transformative.

To agree to a restorative meeting takes courage. Despite all the preparation, in spite of everything that has been put in place to make it as comfortable as possible, this is likely to be an uncomfortable experience. Like getting teeth pulled, there has to be some sense that the end result will make things better, although before the event, this is largely an act of faith. Walking into the room, there will still be feelings of anxiety, fear and anger, concerns about how they and the other may react – in fact, any number of 'unknowns'.[21] During the assessment process, the practitioner will have worked with everyone to help them identify and lower the internal and external barriers keeping them apart. Through thorough preparation, they will have enabled each person to reach their 'threshold of confidence': the point at which they are prepared to take the risk, to take a step across the divide.

Cartoon 13.1: The threshold of confidence

In life, stuff that requires courage, where we don't know the outcome in advance, where things happen beyond imagining, are often the most rewarding. This is why cases where the practitioner is nervous – usually because one or both parties are starting low on the empathy scale – can end up being more significant and satisfying all round than restorative meetings where the practitioner is supremely confident about the outcome, with everyone starting off high on the empathy scale, keen to make up and make good.

Restorative justice can be quite a journey, and, in fact, journey imagery is commonly used by restorative participants: 'Well done for turning a corner'; 'I've definitely crossed a bridge'; 'I'm moving on';

'You've got a difficult road ahead of you'; 'I'm not going back.' While crime can lead people on either side to lose their identity – they may even derive a new identity from the actions of the other – the restorative journey can take them through the thorny path of denial, guilt and self-blame to finding new identity, new meaning and, ultimately, self-respect and honour. Howard Zehr calls this 'the journey to belonging'.[22] It can also release the stuckness, which in the example of the two sisters mentioned earlier had endured for 15 years. Meeting the man who murdered their brother answered their most pressing questions about the crime. It freed them, from the day following their restorative meeting, from the need for their daily phone calls.

Cartoon 13.2: I always wanted us to share it...

When both are moving, converging, the effect is like that of two raindrops running down a window pane. Having taken separate paths since (before) the crime, one or both may suddenly lurch towards the other, they join and two journeys become one. When Peter Woolf met Will Riley, the man he burgled, in a restorative meeting, their individual experiences of suffering converged unexpectedly into one shared story:

> Suddenly I was feeling his pain. He handed it over to me as though he was saying, 'since you're here, you can share this with me.' And when that happened, all of a sudden I knew

there was no way on this planet I could ever harm another human being the way I'd harmed Will, and thousands like him.[23]

Figure 13.1 maps out this path for the individuals involved, charting the distance travelled. Each stage towards the restorative heart includes the lower stages: we start by looking to our own needs, the focus on the self, and move towards compassion for the self *and* the other. This process of resonant empathy has a dynamic of its own, a magic that takes over, which explains why restorative meetings frequently exceed expectations.

Figure 13.1: Into the heart of restorative justice: increasing levels of 'restorativeness' as the gap closes

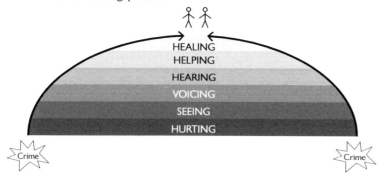

Meaning

> What's more important? A park bench or changing someone's life? (Ray Donovan[24])

People harmed by crime often need to find some meaning or significance in the event. One way that this is frequently expressed is a desire that learning can come from the suffering, from the harm, 'that my pain can prevent someone else's'. Often, this is simply stated as a desire that the person who has caused harm turns a corner and makes the best of their lives. A man who suffered the ultimate loss said to the person who took his son's life: "I want something good to come from my son's death – your son, your future has to be the main focus." A woman whose life was devastated by a burglary said to the man who broke into her house: "Find out what else you can do with your life in a beautiful way." During her restorative meeting, a woman wanted to know all about the background and present circumstances of the man who murdered her husband. She seemed to put the pieces together to form a picture of what might have been behind his actions. On hearing that he had a three-year-old son, she crossed the circle, hugged him and said: "So that something positive can come from this dreadful situation I want you to accept my forgiveness and promise to be a good father to your son."

Ray Donovan, whose son Chris was murdered, took this one step further:

> [Ray] set out to get one of the offenders – an artist – a job and a place on a mentoring programme to become a curator. The man is now working for a charity – Ray is not allowed to say which. 'I called the director and got him a place,' Ray says. 'The secretary who took the call was in tears when she heard the story. Now he's been mentored into the art world as a curator. Isn't that better than him walking the streets? If we go around angry, what kind of example is that to set?', he asks. 'This was the best way we could find to honour Chris. We could have had a park bench made with a plaque on it – or we could do what we are doing. That's the way we look at it. What's more important? A park bench or changing someone's life?'[25]

Ray and Vi's son, Chris, lives on through the work they are doing in prisons and schools to bring about change.

Some people, perhaps those denied a restorative opportunity, seek to find meaning through helping others, by joining or creating campaign or support groups that tackle gangs, domestic violence, sexual offending, homicide or knife crime. This may become their new purpose in life. In this way, if the cycle of crime can be interrupted, their grief is somewhat assuaged. It may also provide an outlet for people, enabling them to shift some of their stuckness by channelling that energy into a more hopeful direction.

Forgiveness

> Authentic forgiveness is a gift of awakening, a freeing of one's spirit, a release of long held toxic energy. Forgiveness is more of a direction than a destination, a way of life grounded in an attitude of humility and compassion. Authentic

> forgiveness has little to do with moral obligations or
> externally imposed values. (Mark Umbreit[26])

Much has been said elsewhere about forgiveness. It is not a word commonly expressed in restorative meetings, and is certainly not one that the practitioner can introduce. I once heard of a practitioner in a restorative meeting saying: "You have heard the apology from so and so ... do you want to forgive him?" This question is definitely *not* in the practice guidance for restorative justice. It makes one wonder what that person replied. However, a restorative meeting can provide a context and opportunity for people to ask for or offer forgiveness, if they choose.

Forgiveness is the prerogative of the forgiver. It is never an obligation and has to be given freely, if at all. The practitioner must honour the journey that participants are choosing, and it will be harmful to make people who may not be inclined or ready to forgive feel somehow inadequate or wrong if they find that they are unable to. For Jo Berry whose father was killed in the Brighton bomb in 1987, 'the idea that if you don't forgive, you're somehow less of a person is not true and it's one of the reasons that I don't use the word'.[27]

Some people can never forgive. Some stress that until the person responsible can prove that he or she has changed their ways, forgiving them lets them off the hook or even condones their wrongdoing.

Sometimes, people are able to forgive the most dreadful wrongs almost immediately. There was a very powerful interview on the television news some years ago with the mother of a boy who had been killed, literally hours earlier, by someone wielding an ice axe. This courageous woman said clearly, "I forgive whoever did this to my son." Her dignity was striking and deeply impressive, unlike the bumbling attempts by the reporter to question her along the usual lines – the media simply didn't know what to make of her stance. I doubt many could do the same. What is certain is that this wonderful reflexive gesture, freely offered in unthinkable circumstances, was the start, not the end, of her journey to forgiveness. Wilma Derksen, whose daughter was murdered, writes movingly about the pros and cons of instant forgiveness:

> For Cliff and I there were some very real disadvantages in
> coming out with a statement about wanting to forgive so
> early in our grief, mainly the misunderstandings around our
> stance. Some folks feared that we were forgiving too early
> and that we might stifle the natural process of grief. Others

thought that we were making a judgement on anyone who expressed anger or that we were being dismissive of any justice-making processes. Still others assumed that our response was made out of weakness, that it was less than sincere, that we were definitely in denial. Some even accused us of not loving our daughter enough to demand justice. But there were also many advantages. Our statement of forgiveness served almost as a mission statement throughout the grieving process. It gave us a destination. It informed those who wanted to support us of where we intended to go and became a rallying point for those who were struggling with the same issues. It helped us to re-engage in life quickly at a time when we didn't have much time to lose. We had two other small children who needed our attention and love; we didn't have the energy for hate. It also allowed us to move the aftershock of violence from the woundedness of our hearts to the saner and safer places in our mind, which are more capable of understanding the complexities of the issues. But, even as I write this, I know that after 22 years into the journey, it still isn't over.[28]

Occasionally, the person responsible will ask for forgiveness during a restorative meeting. They know that only those they have hurt have this power in their gift: to forgive them, to let them go. This request to be absolved is a complete reversal of the power balance. In one meeting, when the person responsible asked "Will you forgive me?", the person whom they had harmed ignored the question. Perhaps thinking they might not have been heard, the person responsible tried once more: "Will you forgive me?" Again, the question was ignored and the word was not used again – even in the informal chat over refreshments. Afterwards, everyone expressed satisfaction with the restorative meeting, and the question of why forgiveness was not forthcoming was left unanswered.

Archbishop Desmond Tutu has said that forgiveness is ultimately an act of self-interest. There may be a deep and urgent need for people to forgive – and they may not be able to wait until the person responsible for harming them can prove that they have changed. We have seen how crime can create a great knot of entanglement between those involved. Forgiveness may help to loosen the cord for those harmed, undoing the ties that bind them with the offence and the offender, releasing everyone from 'walking the treadmill of the past':[29]

Without the experience of forgiveness, without this closure, the wound festers and takes over our lives. It, and the offender, are in control. To forgive a person is to let go. It is to say that I will not define myself by your actions towards me. I will not allow you to have any power over me.[30]

In reconciling what happened, forgiveness can unblock the future. For those harmed, forgiveness allows them to free up the hold that the incident has had over them, softening pain, melting away guilt, dissolving shame, removing blame. With forgiveness, people can let go of their grievances, the desire for revenge, their grudges and their hatred – both for self and other – which may have been gnawing away at their insides. Kim Book, whose daughter was murdered by a young man of 16, wrote in her local newspaper: 'Forgiving LeVaughn has set me free. When we forgive someone, it ends. It puts a stop to the anger we feel. It's over. We are then free to live our lives in peace.'[31] Perhaps this is why people who find that they can forgive often have better health outcomes than those who cling on to their pain.[32]

Although, for some, the idea of forgiveness is founded in religious faith, which can be a huge support through their restorative journey, this feeling that anger and hatred 'eats you up' may be felt both by people of faith and those without, and while the word 'forgiveness' does have a special religious connotation, it can find a wider relevance in the aftermath of a crime.

Forgiveness does not bring an instant end to the pain, loss and grief that remain from more serious offences; it is neither a quick fix nor an easy answer. Saying 'I forgive you' may be just a marker on a longer journey to forgiveness, which will have hidden and difficult depths.

However, just saying the words can bring relief, freeing both parties from the bondage of the crime, providing some level of healing for those who give and receive it. Joanna Nodding writes about reaching forgiveness during the restorative meeting with the man who raped her:

> As the meeting was finishing, I was asked if there was anything else I wanted to say, and I gave him what I've later come to think of as a 'gift'. I said to him 'I forgive you for what you did to me. Hatred just eats you up, and I want you to go on and have a successful life. If you haven't already forgiven yourself, then I hope in the future you will.' I didn't say it to excuse what he did, or to minimise it, but because I wanted myself to be free of that burden

of grievance, and, as importantly for me, I hoped he could learn, move on and forgive himself.[33]

Coming at the end of a restorative meeting after both have had a chance to tell their story and hear the other's in full, this is informed, authentic forgiveness.

Healing

Most crime occurs on a physical level – assault, theft, damage, loss – which can lead to emotional and mental consequences for those harmed as they absorb the shock of what happened. Many people are highly resilient and recover well even if their crime was traumatic. More serious cases can lead to post-traumatic stress (PTS), the symptoms of which are associated with incidents involving 'loss of control, being unable to stop a bad experience from happening, fear of serious injury or death, and not knowing when the experience will end'.[34] PTS can be very complex, and the longer it is left unrecognised and untreated, the more likely it is that the individual will develop maladaptive coping strategies. It can lead to feelings of shame and excessive self-blame, addictive behaviours, difficulties with relationships, dissociation, anxiety, depression, and suicidal thoughts.[35]

People suffering from PTS need help, although, in some cases, even specialist trauma counselling and body work may not be enough. The crime has left too much unfinished business. Many of the symptoms of PTS reveal the persistence of an unhealthy connection with the offence and with the person who harmed them. Through flashbacks, they relive the experience as if it was happening now. Unexpected incidents or objects associated with the crime trigger the original feelings of distress. Hyper-alertness tells them that the threat is still there, and panic attacks release a flood of adrenaline in readiness for a fight or flight response. Obsessive compulsive rituals and self-harming are an attempt to regain the control that was lost during the offence.

A further symptom of PTS is avoidance: efforts to avoid thoughts, feelings, activities, situations and people that bring a reminder of the trauma. For some, the realisation may dawn that without a resolution, avoidance doesn't work, and the shadow of the experience will continue to haunt in some form or other even years after the crime. Releasing the emotional memories from such a powerful and traumatic event – in a safe place – offers at least a chance for healing.[36] Having met the man who raped her, Claire Chung reflected that 'the restorative meeting was the ONLY thing (for me) that kept the fear contained within real boundaries and could then be integrated within the PTSD [post-traumatic stress disorder] treatment.'[37] Linda Dyne, who met her son's killer, said that meeting the person behind the crime was 'incredibly healing … I think anger and all sorts of horrible emotions can eat you up if you let them and it can really stunt you moving on.'[38]

We don't often think of restorative work in the context of health, but perhaps it is no surprise that research shows that restorative justice can bring positive health benefits. For those with serious trauma, research has found that 'victims suffer less intense post-traumatic stress symptoms after face-to-face restorative justice, returning to work and normal life sooner than they do without it'.[39] In their report, Sherman and Strang point out that PTS in military veterans is associated with higher risks of coronary disease. Although the evidence isn't there yet, it is only a matter of time before we can say with confidence that restorative justice is good for the heart.

Even for those without PTS, harbouring grudges, ill will, guilt and rage can make them ill. In a 10-year follow-up to a randomised experiment involving people who had experienced relatively minor crimes in Canberra, Dr Heather Strang from Cambridge University found that there were big differences in anxiety, anger, revenge and fear of crime between those who had been through restorative justice and those in a control group. Higher numbers of the people who had experienced restorative justice could scarcely remember the crime, while significantly more in the control group remember the crime and court vividly. Few were still suffering symptoms of post-traumatic stress, but of those who were, twice as many were in the control group compared with the restorative justice group.[40] Restorative justice allows people to move on and recover over the long term.

Restorative justice recognises that it isn't only those harmed who are suffering. We saw in Chapter One that people who offend have frequently experienced trauma themselves, even if this is unacknowledged. Healing requires a recognition of trauma. This may become obvious as everyone's stories unfold, or it may be at a more subliminal, unconscious level that the connection is made. Perhaps it occurs in the gaps in the process: the exchanged glances while the practitioner is speaking; the pauses; the lulls into silence; the unrelated chatter over refreshments afterwards. The practitioner is trained not to disturb these moments: to become invisible, remain still, perhaps to look at his or her shoes, move slightly out of the circle, go and fetch the tea. To the participants who are focused on one another, the practitioner might almost have left the room, although their non-conspicuous presence maintains the feeling of safety.

———

Healing is non-verbal, not thought through and certainly not planned or anticipated. It may be expressed and received in a look, a touch, a handshake, a smile, a kind word and, sometimes, a hug. When people enter a room fearful, fully expecting to be shouted at or even punched, and when those same people are so moved that they end up hugging each other, a level of healing surely comes to both. Each has found, through compassion for their shared suffering, a shared outlet for their pain. The restorative journey has led them back towards each other, overcoming their fear and vulnerability with great courage.

At the moment of healing, there is connection (or reconnection) but no longer emotional and psychological entanglement. There is no gap. The burning questions that may have haunted one or both parties for months or years are resolved or become irrelevant; the fear, anger, shame and guilt evaporates:

> Ten years on from Christopher's death, Ray and Vi have not only let go of their anger – but in an extraordinary show of compassion, they have managed to forgive the thugs that beat their son to death. In a moment of heart-wrenching humanity that brings tears to the eyes, Ray says that when one of the offenders entered the room, all he wanted to do was hug him. 'I held my hands out to him and he came to me and hugged me,' Ray says. 'He grabbed hold of me and wouldn't let go. He cried and cried,' Ray says. 'As I cuddled him, he whispered "I'm sorry" in my ear. Then he turned to Vi and said simply, "May I?" Vi nodded, and he went to hug her too. He said "sorry," again and again. We said "I forgive you."'[41]

This moment of healing may be the culmination of a long journey – 10 years in Ray and Vi's case. Howard Zehr talks about a healing justice leading to 'wholeness'. The division and brokenness that was within the perpetrator, and which they, in turn, inflicted on others, is made whole:

> with the eyes of knowing
> I move from us and them
> our differences disappear
> the unity of humanity remains
> bridges can be built. (Jo Berry[42])

Wholeness brings inner peace: a knowing and acceptance that we are all human beings, that we are not separate even from those who have harmed us.

It doesn't follow that we are suddenly best buddies with the person who caused us harm, or whom we harmed (although this can happen on occasion). After a restorative meeting, the participants may never want to see each other again. In the hours and days that follow, they may not quite believe what happened, what they have done. It may also be difficult to express their experience to friends and loved ones who weren't there, who didn't share the journey, haven't found the peace it can bring. How can you explain how you came to hug someone who, at the start of the meeting, may have been a complete stranger, perhaps someone to fear – or even your enemy. People who have been there may not quite believe it, but few express regret.

Sometimes, there is healing for one person and not the other. In these cases, the two journeys remain separate, one moving and the other remaining unmoved. The one who 'moves' may find that by giving, even if they get nothing back, they are still able to receive healing.

Reintegration

One of the unique features of restorative justice is the bringing together of people where the agenda is to release a harmful connection caused by a brief and shocking event that may have changed all their lives irrevocably. Some offences involve people already known to one another, belonging perhaps to the same social group, neighbourhood or family. In hate crimes, the person harmed was targeted specifically because they are different – their race, religion or belief, gender identity, sexual orientation, or disability – or even simply their physical size, hair colour, accent or fashion choice. In cases involving gangs and serious group violence, the difference might be a postcode, drug-dealing patch or football team. In random crimes such as robbery, car theft or burglary, there may be no previous connection, and those sitting opposite one another in a restorative meeting come from totally different backgrounds, unlikely to have met in any other context. At its best, as the gap closes, the restorative process can enable these broader social divisions to disappear, bringing significant benefit to community relations.

Reintegration is often achieved over refreshments at the end of the meeting. Restorative practitioners will have many tales to tell: people walking off together after their restorative meeting, sometimes sharing phone numbers so that they can keep in touch; people who previously never spoke greeting one another every time they meet; a spontaneous invitation for the other party to 'come round for a cup of tea'; a person responsible being offered a job by the person they harmed. Not uncommonly, the situation after the crime is better than existed before. People who might otherwise have had little or nothing to do with one another have now met in an intimate situation: social divisions are reduced, stigma and stereotypes broken down and respect is restored. There is a level of healing for the community.

Labels and divisions – 'victim', 'offender', 'innocent', 'guilty', 'good person', 'bad person' – often drop away. The experience hasn't gone away, but it can be integrated into people's lives, while participants find an identity beyond a label and the community welcomes them back as citizens worthy of compassion and respect. Stephen, one of the young men who murdered Ray and Vi's son, Christopher, reflected on the restorative meeting:

> When Ray and Vi told me they forgive me it meant everything. It meant that they understood that what had happened to Christopher was an incident that never should have occurred. Hearing them give me permission to have the best life that I can made me feel like a human again, a good person, with a clear focus and a positive future. I owe that to Christopher. Meeting Ray and Vi has helped me to accept that I owe it to myself too. When I committed this offence I was lost with no direction or purpose. That is no longer the case.[43]

Tracy met Mark, the young man who burgled her house. During their restorative meeting, an agreement was made that he would help her on her allotment as reparation. Reflecting back later, she commented: 'I don't think of him as the burglar, I think of him as Mark.'[44] Towards the end of another restorative meeting, the person who had been harmed said: "Don't define yourself as an offender – you are better than that – and coming to this meeting proves it."

The gap within the individual may also be closed. A common motivation for people who have caused harm is to make the people they love (their parents, partners, children) proud of them. Restorative justice requires courage – the courage to be open, to be vulnerable, to face the unknown. Finding that courage can help restore people's own inner pride and self-worth. One young man came out of his restorative meeting saying, "I felt 10 feet tall!"; another commented: "It's the best thing I've ever done. I would say it was the turning point of my life." People often excel themselves in restorative meetings, overcoming trepidation with daring, which can bring self-forgiveness and self-acceptance. In this way, the restorative meeting can be an important personal project, enabling each individual to learn how to live with themselves.

There is a nice coda to the story in Chapter Two (page 34) shared by the colleague who was burgled by someone who had done casual gardening work for her. She had noticed that after the burglary, she'd been avoiding town, dreading a chance meeting and an awkward exchange. She was later invited into a restorative process and was able to have that encounter in a carefully prepared and managed meeting. Some months after the meeting, she walked past him one day in town, and as she realised who it was, she stopped, turned around and went back. She had a positive conversation about how he was getting on and he asked about her, too. He was extremely grateful and touched that she had taken the time to come back and had not just pretended that she hadn't seen him.

For the person harmed, the fear that may have stopped them going out, visiting town, going to the park, feeling relaxed in their own neighbourhood can lift, allowing them to reclaim their lives, their well-being, their happiness.

Restoration

Restorative justice can help shift the balance back from bad to good, and may go some way to rebuilding what has been damaged in a crime. Sometimes, complete restoration – of damaged property or fractured relationships – really is possible; as one person reflected after their meeting, "It feels like we have come full circle." More often, particularly in the case of serious crimes, even restorative justice can't restore the past. The term 'restorative' then becomes a misnomer. Restorative meetings in serious cases are unlikely to fully meet everyone's needs – and this would, in any case, be impossible in crimes involving disablement or death, where losses can never be recovered.

Crime can be life-changing for those harmed. The old sense of living in a secure, caring and benign world is gone. When you are deliberately hurt, you lose your innocence, and your old, safe, familiar ground is swept away. As Susan Miller puts it: 'Events throw you unwillingly into uncharted places that are unscripted, unimaginable and painful.'[45] New ground has to be found. For some, life will always be divided: time before the crime; time after the crime.

Restorative justice can't restore the past, but it can help in building a better future. A restorative meeting can shift the stuckness. It can lift the negative energy, end the ceaseless ruminating over what happened, provide restoration 'to our full potential as relational beings who flourish when accorded equal concern, respect and dignity'.[46] Reassurances and agreements can stop people living in fear and ameliorate or clear completely the symptoms of PTS – the flashbacks, the triggers, the nightmares. Furthermore, just as the ripples of harm from the crime spread out to affect everyone within the orbit of the perpetrator and the person harmed, positive waves of healing and restoration now wash over their families, friends and communities.

Reducing the gap can lead to a release of these burdens, which, in some cases, can remove a shadow that would otherwise blight lives. A woman who had felt broken by her experience of being burgled by a close neighbour spoke afterwards about the impact of her restorative meeting: "It was like night and day." Vi Donovan said after meeting one of the boys who killed Chris: "It's like a weight has been lifted off us … I came out smiling like I'd just won the pools. We actually hugged him. I whispered 'Thank you.'" Chris won't be brought back, Ray and Vi's old world can never be restored, but their experience helped them to move on from the past, to find their new ground.

With that hug, the handshake – the wonderful story from death row where a man and his victim touched hands on either side of the security glass[47] – the last of the gap is closed, physically and often emotionally, too.

Closure

> I left the meeting feeling 'on top of the world' and for me,
> it was closure. It has allowed me to move forward and know
> that I really am a survivor of a serious crime. (Jo Nodding[48])

Like forgiveness, closure is not a concept that can be introduced by the practitioner. Howard Zehr suggests that the word itself can be offensive, particularly to people who have suffered grave crimes, implying that 'all can be put behind and the book closed, and that is not possible'.[49] However, it is not uncommon for the term to be expressed by participants of restorative meetings.

Closure implies that the situation is finished and it's time to move on. Things may never be the same, but there is the prospect of an end to the suffering caused by the crime: a time when what happened no longer has power over those involved. In the words of a woman who had been attacked in her own home: "It lays a ghost to rest." The person responsible may find that some of the weight has been lifted, may find peace in knowing that they did what they could to undo the harm they caused. For those harmed, the person responsible no longer has any control over their lives. They don't have to fear that this person will hurt them again, and feel hopeful that he or she will make better choices in future. Perhaps closure can only come about when the gap itself is allowed to close, as far as it is able to.

Some people manage to integrate the harmful experience into their lives, put it in its proper place, as a powerful memory that strengthens but doesn't define them. Some may never be able to draw a line under it; that longing may never be extinguished. They may carry photographs of those they lost, scars that won't heal, injuries that remind them of the crime because they see them in the mirror every day.

Some remain locked into things, stuck in their stories. They feel justified, self-righteous, unable to melt their anger and hatred, which they can defend entirely, and which no one can judge. Some have adopted the identity of being 'victim' or 'offender' to the extent that they are completely defined by their label, their story, and find that it serves a purpose for them (even if it is nasty). The practitioner may wish to liberate them from this mental trap, but until they are ready to own it as theirs, to just feel those emotions and not be vindicated or imprisoned by what happened, they may not be ready to take that step. Barbara Tonge writes: 'It is natural not to want to be healed, initially ... hurting counts. Prolonged hurting can become a pre-occupation, blocking recovery, sapping strength, fuelling anger and draining all channels of activity.'[50] They don't want to find closure, to move on – yet.

Afterwards

Care must be taken in the sensitive time after a restorative meeting. People who found that they melted unexpectedly may take time to process what happened, may leave feeling emotionally exposed and vulnerable. In the cold light of day, they may not quite believe what they did. In cases where there has been a death, relatives of the deceased may experience feelings of guilt and betrayal if they found themselves unexpectedly liking the person who killed their loved one. Everyone will need sensitive understanding, support and aftercare. The role of their own support network is critical at this stage.

The practitioner will aim to meet all parties in person to check in with them. This may typically entail a phone call on the evening of the meeting, with a follow-up meeting a week later. Experience indicates that the person responsible is particularly likely to experience a 'dip' in emotion after the meeting. Feelings continue to change over time, and the practitioner will visit as often and for as long as participants need. Dr Mark Walters of Sussex University, who has researched restorative justice in cases involving hate crime, comments: 'This aspect of Restorative Justice was one of the key findings from my research. The fact that practitioners made contact periodically post conference was a great relief to the victim, who felt cared about.'[51]

In most cases, one restorative meeting is as much as participants want. In some instances, further restorative meetings are requested. This may be particularly helpful in reviewing whether outcomes and agreements have been met. One participant was left still doubting the sincerity of the person she had met, and the restorative meeting was followed up with an exchange of letters. Tylah, the young man who met Linda, whose house he burgled (see Chapter Ten), started a correspondence with Linda's seven-year-old daughter, Olivia. Tylah had cried during the restorative meeting with Linda as she described searching for days along the lanes near her house for letters and keepsakes from her kids, which he had carelessly discarded after the burglary. Tylah wrote to Olivia to apologise, promising to pay back her birthday money, which he had taken. Olivia replied: 'I hope you will never have to go back [to prison] because I think you are a nice person and I forgive you even if you don't give me your money back.' Both still correspond, and Linda believes that the experience has had a huge impact on Tylah, and provided a valuable life lesson to Olivia.[52]

Ideally, the outcomes from the restorative process, forged in a meeting when there was a high level of goodwill, will inform a programme of support for all sides and particularly for the person responsible, by addressing the wider set of needs that led him or her into trouble. Here, a golden opportunity for what might be a life change must not be missed. The meeting may offer a strong motivation for change, which may or may not be articulated in a written contract. If this chance is allowed to slip, not only does it undo much of the benefit of the restorative process, but it may lead to further offending, future victims.

Sometimes, even after the restorative process has been completed, the crime is repeated. Sometimes, the person harmed will oscillate, go backwards, hold on to their rage and bitterness, as well as their empathy, or simply feel ambivalent about the whole process. Empathy is not linear, and while it is difficult not to consider the whole process a failure, it is perhaps not surprising if there isn't an instant and lasting transformation of deep-rooted patterns. Changing habits is hard and few of us learn life's lessons first time round. The practitioner will also be keen to reflect continually on their practice and, like their clients, to learn from their own mistakes.

Notes

[1] Zehr, H. (2002) 'Journey to Belonging', in E. Weitekamp, and H. Kerner (eds) *Restorative Justice: Theoretical Foundations*, Abingdon: Willan Publishing, p 28.

[2] Why Me? is an organisation that campaigns for victims of crime to have access to restorative justice (www.why-me.org/

[3] Braithwaite, J. (1989) *Crime, shame and reintegration*, Cambridge: Cambridge University Press.

[4] Braithwaite, J. (1989) *Crime, shame and reintegration*, Cambridge: Cambridge University Press, p 55.

[5] Braithwaite, J. (1989) *Crime, shame and reintegration*, Cambridge: Cambridge University Press, p 100.

[6] Brown, B. (2012) *Daring greatly, how the courage to be vulnerable transforms the way we live, love, parent and lead*, London: Penguin, p 72.

[7] Ahmed, E., Harris, J., Braithwaite, J. and Braithwaite, V. (2001) *Shame management through reintegration*, Cambridge: Cambridge University Press.

[8] Gilligan, J. (1996) *Violence, our deadly epidemic and its causes*, New York, NY: Grosset/Puckman Books, p 110.

[9] Sherman, L. and Strang, H. (2000) 'Recidivism patterns in the Canberra Re-integrative shaming experiments (RISE)', Centre for Restorative Justice Research School of Social Sciences, Australian National University.

[10] Morris, A. (2001) 'Revisiting reintegrative shaming', *Criminology Aotearoa/ New Zealand*, no 16, p 12.

[11] Woolf, P. (2008) *The damage done*, London: Bantam Books, p 307.

[12] Harris, N., Walgrave, L. and Braithwaite, J. (2004) 'Emotional dynamics in restorative conferences', *Theoretical Criminology*, vol 8, no 2, p 193.

[13] Brown, B. (2012) *Daring greatly, how the courage to be vulnerable transforms the way we live, love, parent and lead*, London: Penguin, p 69.

---

[14] Brown, B. (2012) *Daring greatly, how the courage to be vulnerable transforms the way we live, love, parent and lead*, London: Penguin, pp 185-6.

[15] Restorative Justice Council (2013) 'Kelvin's story', *Resolution*, no 47, pp 10–11.

[16] Miller, S. (2011) *After the crime*, New York, NY: New York University Press, p 127.

[17] David Doerfler was the founder of the victim–offender dialogue programme in Texas described in Miller (2011) *After the crime*, New York, NY: New York University Press, p 229. This motivational statement is used in the preparation material for the offenders.

[18] See, for example, the lecture by Carlen, P. (October 2012) Against Rehabilitation; For Reparative Justice in *Crime, justice and social democracy*, pp 89–104 (www.palgraveconnect.com/pc/doifinder/10.1057/9781137008695.0016).

[19] Kathleen, quoted in 'The conversation', *The Guardian*, 21 May 2011.

[20] Walters, M. (2014) *Hate crime and restorative justice: Exploring causes, repairing harms*, Oxford: Oxford University Press.

[21] "There are known knowns; there are things we know that we know. There are known unknowns; that is to say, there are things that we now know we don't know. But there are also unknown unknowns – there are things we do not know we don't know." (Statement to the press by US Secretary of Defense, Donald Rumsfeld in 2002)

[22] Zehr, H. (2000) 'Journey to belonging', paper presented at the Fourth International Conference on Restorative Justice for Juveniles, October (Tübingen, Germany) (www.restorativejustice.org/articlesdb/articles/2279).

[23] http://theforgivenessproject.com/stories/peter-woolf-will-riley-england/

[24] http://tinyurl.com/og56npf

[25] http://tinyurl.com/og56npf

[26] Umbreit, M. (2009) 'Authentic forgiveness', Regents of the University of Minnesota, Centre for Restorative Justice & Peacemaking, School of Social Work, College of Education & Human Development.

[27.] Spencer, G. (ed) *Forgiving and remembering in Northern Ireland: Approaches to conflict resolution*, London: Continuum, p 226.

[28.] Extract from 'We will forgive you' by Wilma Derksen (unpublished). I heard Wilma speak at a conference in Toronto in 2006, and this quote was made at the time, before the man who murdered her daughter was charged in 2007 and convicted of her murder in 2011. For an updated story of Wilma's journey through the trial, visit: http://theforgivenessproject.com/?s=wilma&post_type=stories. Wilma also gave a TED lecture 'When polarity in forgiveness happens' (www.youtube.com/watch?v=U7Byq9sW_XU), and she is in the last stages of finishing her book, 'Tension of truth', that she says 'completes our story'.

[29.] Richard Holloway, quoted in Cherry, S. (2012) *Healing agony*, London: Continuum Books, p 5.

[30.] Zehr, H. (1989) *Changing lenses*, Scottdale, PA: Herald Press, p 47.

[31.] Book, K. (1997) 'Living free in an unforgiving world', *Delaware State News*, 30 March, quoted in Miller, S. (2011) *After the crime*, New York, NY: New York University Press.

[32.] See, for example, Van Oyen Witvliet, C., Ludwig, T. and Vander Laan, K. (2001) 'Granting forgiveness or harboring grudges: implications for emotion, physiology, and health', *Psychological Science*, vol 12, no 2, pp 117–23; Lawler-Row, K.A, Karremans, J.C., Scott, C., Edlis-Matityahou, M. Edwards, L. (2008) 'Forgiveness, physiological reactivity and health: the role of anger', *International Journal of Psychophysiology*, vol 68, no 1, pp 51–8. Both studies indicate that people who are able to forgive have less stress and lower heart rates.

[33.] Nodding, J. (2011) 'Jo's story', *Resolution* #40 (see also Video Resources in Appendix).

[34.] Wallis, P. (2010) *Are you okay?*, London: Jessica Kingsley Publishers, p 113.

[35.] Rothschild, B. (2000) *The body remembers: The psychophysiology of trauma and trauma treatment*, New York, NY: W.W. Norton & Company.

[36.] See Rugge, T. and Scott, T.-L. (2009) *Restorative justice's impact on participants' psychological and physical health*, User Report 2009-03, Ottawa: Public Safety Canada.

[37.] Extract from personal correspondence, published with permission.

———

[38.] www.stuff.co.nz/national/crime/9247211/Meeting-criminals-helps-the-healing

[39.] Sherman, L. and Strang, H. (2007) *Restorative justice: The evidence*, London: The Smith Institute, p 14.

[40.] Heather Strang, University of Cambridge, from a presentation to the 'Restoring the Balance' Conference at St Catherine's College, Oxford, 28 November 2013, entitled: 'Victims and restorative justice: what do we know from international research evidence?' Heather's research findings are available at: www.criminologysymposium.com/download/18.4dfe0028139 b9a0cf4080001566/

[41.] http://tinyurl.com/og56npf

[42.] Extract from 'Bridges can be built' by Jo Berry (lifeafterhate.org/2012/02/bridges-can-be-built/).

[43.] Extract from a letter written by Stephen, one of the young men who murdered Christopher Donovan, in 'Restorative justice — what it meant to me' (www.chrisdonovantrust.org/restorative-justice.php).

[44.] This quote is an extract from one of four brief videos about restorative justice that are well worth viewing; see 'Behind the Hoodie' (https://vimeo.com/23797353).

[45.] Miller, S. (2011) *After the crime*, New York, NY: New York University Press, p 3.

[46.] Archibold, B. and Llewellyn, J. (2006) 'The challenges of institutionalising comprehensive restorative justice: theory and practice in Nova Scotia', *Dalhousie Law Journal*, vol 29, pp 257–343, at pp 305–6.

[47.] I heard this extraordinary story from the (recently retired) restorative justice trainer Kenneth Webster.

[48.] Nodding, J. (2011) 'Jo's story', *Resolution*, no 40, p 7.

[49.] Zehr, H. (2002) *The little book of restorative justice*, Intercourse, PA: Good Books, p 71.

[50.] 'Barbara Tonge reflects on bereavement in the wake of her daughters death' (http://thefriend.org/article/thought-for-the-week-healing-not-hurting/).

[51.] Mark Walter's research into restorative justice in cases of hate crime has been published: Walters, M. (2014) *Hate crime and restorative justice: Exploring causes, repairing harms*, Oxford: Oxford University Press.

[52.] Restorative Justice Council (2013) 'Linda's story', *Resolution*, Autumn, p 10.

Conclusion

Why is restorative justice so special? Often, the people involved meet only twice in their lives. The first time was out of control, full of hurt. At the next meeting, both are reaching out, trying to connect with one another across the gap. Restorative justice uses the energy unleashed from the crime to lift people upwards from the lower levels of empathy, where the focus is on the self, to the higher levels, where the focus is also on the other. Empathy is not only about trying to understand the other person's world; it is also about communicating that understanding to that person. Often, the tipping/melting point, when the focus shifts from self to other, when the connection is made, happens at the point during the restorative meeting termed the 'transition stage' exactly for this reason. With the right conditions and a skilful practitioner, the process works by itself, people are pulled closer together knowing that the other person holds the key to their own healing, like subatomic particles that are attracted by an invisible force.

As we have seen, closing the gap is a delicate business. Restorative justice involves a journey with many steps, and it is important to follow each step carefully. Processing and ultimately letting go of something as harmful as a crime takes time. An instant apology is not going to do it; instant forgiveness and acceptance are not going to do it. Stories have to be told, needs voiced and addressed. Both parties must forgive themselves to move forward. Restorative justice provides a safe space for this communication, encouraging a willingness to grapple with difficult emotions, to explore uncomfortable needs and seek consensus on a way forward.

Crime is dehumanising. It is an invasion of our lives, wrenches away our control and damages our sense of self. Every crime involves a breach of one or other of the shared values or principles that make society work, which have been translated over time into our code of law. We are usually unaware of how strongly we hold those values until someone violates them, when we are shocked and outraged. As a response to crime, restorative justice is re-humanising, appeals to our common humanity and rebuilds lives through the 'lost art of explanation, consideration, apology and reintegration'.[1] In the process, restorative justice validates and reinforces many of our core values: of caring and compassion, honesty, responsibility, personal integrity, non-judgement, inclusion, and respect. Some restorative justice scholars start off by describing restorative justice as a set of principles and values, which are then applied in practice – using facilitated communication as a means of repairing the harm caused by crime, restoring damaged relationships and reintegrating the person responsible back into the community.[2] This account began by looking at the practice, describing restorative justice as a 'conversation', allowing its underpinning principles and values to emerge as the story of the process unfolded. Ultimately, though, the practice of restorative justice and the principles and values upon which it is founded are indivisible. Without a deep appreciation of the underlying principles and values of restorative justice, restorative practice has the potential to cause further harm.

With all the challenges facing our world, conflict is inevitable and we urgently need to reinforce our core human values. We also need reminding (or teaching) that we are all connected, that how we behave, react and respond affects everyone else. Pepinsky describes empathy as 'the emotional glue that binds people together in respect and dignity', contrasting empathy with narcissism, which he says results in separation and conflict.[3] Some authors fear that we have raised an entire generation without the prerequisites for developing empathy.[4] Whether or not the person responsible needs a victim empathy course to get them across the starting line, restorative justice is, of itself, an empathy training ground, as every aspect of the restorative process is designed to enhance empathy. Moreover, the material for this restorative justice empathy training is a real–life situation of great significance to those involved. The empathy response has been shown by researchers to be modulated by factors including the situational context in which people meet, the relationship between them and the intensity of the other person's emotions. All of these conditions can fall into place in a restorative meeting, often resulting in rapid movement up the empathy scale from the most unpromising starting point. Baron–Cohen describes empathy as 'one of the most precious (and under–utilised) resources in our world'.[5] A successful restorative meeting nourishes an ability to empathise that spreads out far beyond the specific people sitting across from one another in the room.

The power of restorative justice is best appreciated through stories. A young man was beaten unconscious by the leader of a gang, who accused him of raping the younger sister of one of their group. He dropped out of school, became severely depressed and wouldn't leave his house without his parents. As time passed, the gang leader began to wonder whether the rumour that led to the attack was true, or whether he had been set up for an unnecessary fight with a malicious lie. He started to regret the attack, and although still not 100% certain where the truth lay, he agreed to a restorative meeting, recognising that he shouldn't have got involved and had "gone too far". Having summoned enormous courage to meet his attacker, the young man's need to feel safe was met through an apology and reassurances from the gang leader. He was able to rebuild his life, get an apprenticeship and finally look on the attack as a blessing that made him a stronger person and brought his family closer. Reflecting back on his restorative process, he said: "It had to happen." Hearing the extraordinary accounts from the people whose experiences are shared in this book – Ray and Vi, Claire, Peter, Jo, Sari, Kathleen, Stephen, and many others – it is painful to conceive of these people being denied restorative justice.

True, many restorative meetings are less dramatic and life-changing than the case studies used here – they may be rather more functional than transformative. Although unexciting, they will never feel mundane for those involved. During a meeting between a shopkeeper and a young person who stole a chocolate bar, every aspect of the restorative process is an expression of values. Every restorative encounter nurtures empathy, making the world a more peaceful, a more connected, place.

I'm with the young man, and believe that restorative justice has to happen. People who cause harm have an obligation to repair the harm they have caused. If people harmed wish to be involved in restorative justice – and it will never be everyone's choice – it should be considered their fundamental human right. The research shows clear benefits that justify this approach on the grounds of cost alone. There is no longer any question of 'if', only 'how' and 'when'.

Arguments against restorative justice per se often misunderstand or wilfully misrepresent the process, with talk of a 'soft option' or 'forced apologies'. The recent flurry of interest in restorative justice has also exposed the inconsistency of provision.[6] There are pressing questions about how and when it should be available, and early attempts to embed restorative justice at various points in the criminal justice process have each had their pros and cons. I hope this discussion never ends.

Criminal justice in the UK is entering a world of commissioning services, bringing commercial pressures to reduce costs and consequent fears that this sensitive area of practice, which requires commitment, time and resources, will be watered down. Conversely, quality standards, which are being introduced to safeguard participants, could inadvertently stifle freedom, creativity and innovation. In restorative justice, there is no one model and no best practice; instead, there is emerging practice and continually evolving models of delivery. Providing restorative justice stays true to its core values and principles, diversity can be welcomed and the future of restorative justice should be in safe hands.

In summary, restorative justice recognises that, sooner or later, we are all 'offenders' and 'victims', and in the restorative process, those labels frequently drop away. It challenges the causes of crime and our own roles in maintaining them, pulling down the barriers between us so that we can heal and live together after brokenness. Each crime provides an opportunity to learn, to transform lives, strengthen communities and improve society. By cultivating empathy, restorative justice can bring out the best from the worst aspects of humanity, putting values and empathy back into the criminal justice system by giving it a more restorative heart. It can create a better future.

Notes

[1] Hoyle, C. and Cunneen, C. (2010) *Debating restorative justice*, Oxford: Hart Publishers, p 91.

[2] Zehr, H. and Mika, H. (1998) 'Fundamental concepts of restorative justice', *Contemporary Justice Review*, vol 1, no 1, pp 47–55. Reprinted in *Restorative justice*, Roche, D. (2003) pp 73–81. The International Library of Essays in Law & Legal Theory, Second Series. Aldershot: Dartmouth/Ashgate, Braithwaite, J. (1989) *Crime, shame and reintegration*, Cambridge University Press, Cambridge, and Johnson, G. and Van Ness, D. (eds), (2007) *Handbook of restorative justice*, Willan, Cullumpton, Devon.

[3] Pepinsky, H. (2008) 'Empathy and restoration', in D. Sullivan and L. Tifft (eds) *Handbook of restorative justice. A global perspective*, London and New York, NY: Routledge, pp 188–97.

[4] See, for example, Eissele, I. (2009) *Kalte Kinder: Sie kennen kein Mitgefühl. Sie entgleiten uns*, Freiburg: Herder Verlag Gmbh.

[5] Baron-Cohen, S. (2012) *Zero degrees of empathy*, London: Penguin, p 130.

[6] The HM Inspectorate of Constabulary (HMIC) Joint Inspectorates report published in September 2012 found patchy quality and quantity of restorative justice provision nationally. See Criminal Justice Joint Inspection (2012) 'Facing up to offending: use of restorative justice in the criminal justice system', Joint Inspection Report (www.restorativejustice.org.uk/news/cjji/).

Further information and resources

Further reading

Hopkins, B. (ed) (2015) *Just theories: An exploration of the many ways to understand restorative practice*, London, Jessica Kingsley Publishers.
An exciting new book edited by Belinda Hopkins in which the restorative approach will be examined through a number of psychological and sociological 'lenses' to explore what is happening in the restorative encounter. Belinda has also written several books about restorative practice in schools and care homes.

Liebmann, M. (2007) *Restorative justice: How it works*, London: Jessica Kingsley Publishers.
The perfect guide for anyone wishing to learn about restorative justice. Liebmann clearly outlines the principles of the approach, charting its history and describing, with lots of case examples, its practical application in a range of contexts. Essential reading.

Miller, S. (2011) *After the crime*, New York/London: New York University Press,
This book features remarkable stories of restorative meetings following the most serious of crimes, organised by Victim Voices Heard in Delaware and facilitated by executive director Kim Book.

Partington, M. (2012) *If you sit very still*, Bristol: Vala Publishing.
This is an extraordinary account by Marian Partington of her struggle with grief and rage after she learnt that her sister Lucy, who had been missing for 20 years had been kidnapped, tortured and killed by Fred and Rosemary West, and her determination to find a compassionate response and 'salvage the sacred'.

Potter, H. (2014) *A brief's history of the law*, Woodbridge: Boydell and Brewer
This book will be a history of the English common law expanding on the research Harry Potter did when presenting for the BBC series 'The strange case of the law'.

Wallis, P. and Tudor, B. (2008) *The pocket guide to restorative justice*, London: Jessica Kingsley Publishers.
A book of best practice guidance for restorative practitioners designed to slip into the pocket.

Wallis, P., Aldington, C. and Leibmann, M. (2010) *What have I done? A victim empathy programme for young people*, London: Jessica Kingsley Publishers.
A programme with creative activities and resources for working with young people who have offended designed to encourage and develop empathy.

Walters, M. (2014) *Hate crime and restorative justice: Exploring causes, repairing harms*, Oxford: OUP.
Mark Walters presents the findings from his research into restorative justice and hate crime, using case examples to explore the complex causes and features of hate incidents and the potential for restorative justice to bring benefit in this challenging area of practice.

Wright, M. (1996) *Justice for victims and offenders: A restorative response to crime* (2nd edn), Winchester: Waterside Press; and Wright, M. (1999) *Restoring respect for justice*, Winchester: Waterside Press.
Martin Wright, an early leader in restorative justice and founding member of the Restorative Justice Council has written widely about restorative justice and peacemaking both within the UK and across Europe.

Zehr, H. (1990) *Changing lenses: A new focus for crime and justice*, Scottdale, PA: Herald Press) and Zehr, H. (2002) *The little book of restorative justice*, Intercourse, PA: Good Books.
Howard Zehr is widely regarded as one of the pioneers of restorative justice, and his *Little book of restorative justice* is a real treasure.

Video resources

There are many videos available online, in which people share their experience of restorative justice. Here is a selection with stories from this book:

Jo Nodding: 'The meeting: the story of Jo Nodding': https://vimeo.com/27590008

Peter Woolf and Will Riley 'The Woolf within': www.dailymotion.com/video/xplz5u_the-woolf-within_people

Jo Berry: http://tvapex.com/watch.aspx?i=839&j=Building-Bridges%20for%20Peace&k=search

Ray and Vi Donovan: Restorative Bristol Conference: www.youtube.com/watch?v=WdiT2NMX7Mc

Tracy and Mark: 'Behind the Hoodie': https://vimeo.com/23797353

Websites

Restorative Justice Council

The RJC is the national umbrella organisation for restorative justice. Its website has a selection of case studies (including restorative approaches in non-criminal contexts) and provides information about new developments in restorative approaches, research, resources, quality standards, training opportunities and events.
• www.restorativejustice.org.uk

Restorative Justice Online

Another excellent web-based resource offering a worldwide perspective is Restorative Justice Online, a service provided by the Prison Fellowship International Centre for Justice and Reconciliation.
• www.restorativejustice.org

Why Me?

The Why Me? charity was founded to share the stories of people who have been through a restorative process and drawn huge benefit, to help them to share their experience and encourage others caught up in crime to go down a restorative route.
• www.why-me.org

Transforming Conflict

Transforming Conflict is the national centre for restorative approaches in youth settings, and the website provides a wealth of information about events, news and resources.
• www.transformingconflict.org

Building Bridges for Peace

Jo Berry's story is mentioned in this book. Jo is a wonderful speaker, and both she and Patrick Magee are committed to exploring and promoting non-violent solutions to conflict.
• www.buildingbridgesforpeace.org

Chris Donovan Trust

Ray and Vi Donovan founded the Chris Donovan Trust in honour of their son Christopher who was murdered. Ray and Vi now work tirelessly in schools, youth offending institutions and prisons 'to help people to understand what it is like to be a victim and through that knowledge prevent them from creating more victims.'
• www.chrisdonovantrust.org

Providing support: Protective Behaviours

A programme called Protective Behaviours provides an excellent way of supporting younger people in their recovery. Protective Behaviours was developed in the US in the 1970s in response to an observation that many young people lack the skills to protect themselves from abuse.[1] It is used by the police, youth workers, schools and disability service workers, in residential care services and domestic violence services, and by mediators and counsellors.

Although the most important thing to offer is a listening and believing ear, Protective Behaviours has practical ideas and exercises that an adult supporting a young person can suggest. These help the young person to gain insight into their reaction to the offence, develop strategies to stay safe in future and identify and draw upon their own strengths and personal support network. Protective Behaviours can provide excellent preparation for a restorative process, helping people find the confidence and courage to take the intentional risk of meeting their attacker – which may be the best or only way for them to gain reassurance that they are now safe again. Some areas have dedicated services to support young people affected by crime.[2]

Notes

[1] The programme is outlined in S. Keen et al, *Why me?* (Jessica Kingsley Publishers 2010).

[2] Oxfordshire's service is called SAFE! Support for Young People Affected by Crime (www.safeproject.org.uk).

Index

Please note: page numbers followed by 'n' refer to material in footnotes. 'RJ' refers to restorative justice.

Printed in Great Britain
by Amazon